Letters
never
meant
to be
Read

Volume III

Howard Altman Ditric Marie Bowie Linda O' Connell Jessica Cote
Megan Coyote Marc D. Crepeaux Casey DeMoss Ikechukwu Echebiri
Maryanne Frederick Clara Freeman Wesley J. Ginther Susan Grant
Atreyee Gupta A.M. Hounchell Tamara Herndon Frank Kelly
Josh Lefkowitz C.K. Legrem Kim Lehnhoff Tricia Lowther
Peaches Mothersbaugh Christie Nortje Joshua Ogri Leah Oviedo
Konstantina P. Amol Parikh Tina Rafowitz Jean Reyes Meghan C. Rynn
K. Gail Sease Michael Shawn Sommermeyer B.L. Teague Laura Lee Tingley
Oeun Sieng Un Grace Veritas Sargam Vyas Shelby Yarchin

edited by Marc D. Crepeaux,A.M. Hounchell, and Meghan C. Rynn

VOLUME III

LETTERS NEVER MEANT TO BE READ

Copyright © 2018 Rusty Wheels Media, LLC.

Printed in the United States of America

First Printing, 2018

Rusty Wheels Media, LLC.

P.O. Box 1692

Rome, GA 30162

RUSTY WHEELS MEDIA
THEY KEEP TURNING

ISBN-13: 978-1-7328400-3-4

ISBN-10: 1-7328400-3-2

iii

VOLUME III

LETTERS NEVER MEANT TO BE READ

-Disclaimer- Any resemblance to actual persons, living or dead, events, or locales is entirely coincidental. While some instances or thoughts may appear real, they are merely a perception of reality, brought to life by the letter writer. If you feel you have been wronged somehow as a result of this publication, feel free to write and send a letter of your own.

VOLUME III

LETTERS NEVER MEANT TO BE READ

To know me is to know my pack; my family; my land. I believe in magic and in each person's ability to change the world. Individually, we can be a force of creation—together, we are infinite. Be empowered. Be kind. Be a beacon of truth. And remember, Step 1: Don't Die, because Life is Delicious!

-Megan Coyote

To all the letter writers, past and present. To those yet to take ink to page. I appreciate you all for helping us accomplish this dream.

-Marc

To Charlesa for everything you did.

-A.M.

Remember the teacher who saw through your disguise? The hitchhiker you picked up on that lonely highway? The stranger you shared a seat with on that long flight? Random connections sometimes surprise. Will this one? Let's see!

– Frank Kelly

VOLUME III

For people who light candles and create shadows.

- Tricia Lowther

Water is my writing talisman. Showers, lakes, streams, rivers inspire my creativity, but the ocean pulls on my Midwestern soul with the same intensity the moon tugs the tide. Life lived forward, viewed microscopically in reverse, supplies my humorous, serious, bittersweet essays and poetry.

- Linda O'Connell

To the uniquely common people.

-Oeun

To Marc, for taking a chance. And to my children, for providing me with light when the darkness seemed it would swallow me whole.

- Grace

Your loving daughter.

-Sargam Vyas

For projects past, and this precious book.

Let there be many more in our future . . .

—Marc, RJ&M

VOLUME III

Table of Contents

VOLUME III

VOLUME III

Dear Reader,

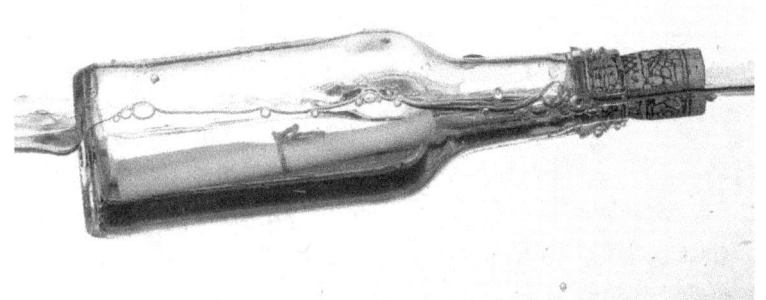

Welcome to the third volume of *Letters Never Meant to be Read*. This is a non-chronological series, so read on without trepidation.

Have you ever wanted to write a letter to

that guy or gal you brushed up against on

the train? How about that lost love, or the

friend who did you wrong?

What started as a wish, a dream, an experiment turned obsession, has become reality, a shared reality. Funny to say, but I must be careful when I declare that I am going to do something. I used to hound both my closest confidants and weary strangers for letters. Now, they come in pairs every day and we cherish them all. This act of reflection and thought is akin to every one of you hav-

1

ing your own personal lighthouse. We know you are there and we see your beacon.

Even those who choose to remain anonymous are given a wonderful opportunity to share with the world their deepest thoughts, wondering hopes, quickening fears, farthest dreams, and burdening sadness. I hope that this offers you, Dear Reader, a glimpse of these emotions and authenticities of our time.

This collection includes pieces from the first ever *Letters Never Meant to be Read Writing Contest*, an idea first brought to light by A.M. Hounchell. We were taken aback by the response as letters came pouring in from all over the world. The other editors and I found it very difficult to choose the winners. The top three are first in this publication. We hope you find them just as worthy of that honor as we did.

It is with great pleasure that I welcome you into this collection, either as a reader, a letter writer, or the future possibility of both. As I said in the beginning of this project, I want nothing more than to continue as the steward of letters and the watchman of words for many years to come.

— Marc

To the Other Parents of Children
at My Daughter's School,

You have no idea, most of you.

It was the Year Five class assembly today. Parents were invited, and I went as usual. I took my place amongst you, gave out the occasional tight smile, even made awkward small talk before the performance. You probably think I'm unfriendly. Quiet. Not in any of the cliques. Not really one of you.

I tried hard not to let my anxiety show, hoped that when she searched me out in the audience, my daughter would see in my face only support, encouragement, and pride.

We put our kids on display, and we clap and cheer them even when they stumble over their lines. But school events are harder for some than others. They don't always build confidence. Sometimes they destroy it.

Reception year was fine. When kids make mistakes at the age of four or five, people think it's cute. My little Marnie was an angel in the nativity. All she had to do was dance. And back then she loved to dance. She stood out, but in a good way.

3

In Year One all the proud parents watched their children's first-class assembly. Only the most confident speakers were given lines, while others held up pictures they'd drawn. Marnie was prompted to hold up her painting. Typically distracted, she held it upside down, but no one really cared. Still cute. She was on the waiting list that year to see the educational psychologist for what her teacher termed 'behavioral issues.'

By Year Two everybody had a line to learn. Marnie practiced at home, shouted to me from the top of the stairs as I encouraged her to speak loudly enough for the whole hall to hear. By then the school had called in the Autism and Social Communication team. I was baffled. I knew she was different from other kids, she struggled with some things, could be difficult, but Autism? That year she missed her line; the other kids skipped over her and carried on like she wasn't there.

Age seven she tried again. I told her it didn't matter, that she wasn't to worry. Her turn came and she stood, screwed up her scarlet face, grunted, and made those odd jerky arm movements that mean she's in distress. The hall shrank into a tight knot of tension. She held my eyes and let out a squeal of frustration. When the next child stood up, relief swept the room. Marnie twisted in her seat until it was over. I waited until I got to the car before I cried.

Last year, Marnie was the only kid who wasn't given a line, a fact I'm sure none of you even noticed. I sat and watched your children recite their parts; the shy kids,

4

the confident kids, the average, and the only one who didn't say a thing. I was there.

Then today. She'd learned her part, just one short sentence. Chloe, who sat next to her, had several lines. I told Marnie just to stand and say the words, that she didn't have to look at anyone's face. Her turn came. Chloe had spoken the line before hers in a clear, confident voice. Marnie stood and twisted her hands together. Red-faced, she turned to the curtains and quickly mumbled her words, then sat. The next child stood.

I was the proudest parent in the room. I'm sure some of you will have compared your child's performance to Marnie's, and thought at least yours wasn't the worst. I'm sure, if you thought about it, you'd all say your child did better than mine. But you're wrong.

It takes more guts for a child with social difficulties to stand up and speak than it does for a naturally confident child. Marnie has had to be brave. Every school day that passes without incident is a victory. She's had to deal with sensory issues; not being able to stand the small noises other people hardly notice, being distracted by smells and textures. To actually make her mouth say the words that are in her head is a real struggle. It's like there's this clamp holding her jaw shut. She wants to speak, but she just, can't. I know. I don't resent your children for their easy won successes; I wish mine found things as easy. But Marnie has taught me to look at the world differently. I've had to learn patience. One of the hardest things is wanting to help but knowing that what I think of as 'help' might not be what's best. I've learned to praise effort, not results.

Chloe was the star of the show today, praised for doing what comes naturally to her. But Marnie's 'bad' performance was the result of overcoming huge internal barriers. Invisible barriers. Barriers that kids like Chloe never have to face, that most people never even think about. Marnie did better than clever, confident Chloe, because Marnie achieved something, even if none of the rest of you saw it. I don't expect you to love or understand my daughter. You have your own problems, your own story, different things to worry about, but, please, don't dismiss her as that weird kid. Don't let your kids exclude her, and don't treat her any differently from the others either. She hates to be treated differently. She's unparalleled at detecting the merest hint of condescension.

I can't make your kids invite Marnie to their parties. I can't force them to be patient when they don't understand why she doesn't just speak up. But maybe you could tell them that the quietest kids can be full of surprises. If they gave her a chance, they'd know that Marnie is bright, honest, funny, and fiercely loyal. It's easy to tell kids to be kind and to respect difference, harder for them to know what that means in practice. Maybe you could tell them that persevering through difficulty says more about a person than doing what comes easy. And that the hard work it takes to build a relationship with someone who struggles with communication is more than worth the effort.

Marnie's Mum

VOLUME III

Dear Rapist,

Ten years have passed since that night. Me laughing with my friends. Your crooked smile leering. My girlfriend thought you were "just soooo hot!!!" She hated me for your attentions. I hated myself, too.

I guess you knew I wasn't into it. Not that it mattered. Your fingers on my back made me shiver when you handed me my glass. I felt so daring, so mature; out drinking cocktails with college boys. Well, boys old enough to go to college. I never did bother to ask if you were actually enrolled.

The syrupy sweet covered the taste of the Vodka nicely. You failed to mention it was covering other things as well. My girlfriend called out to us to come smoke a bowl. I sat beside her. You sat beside me. I remember I wanted to move, but it seemed rude so I stayed — your thoughts pressed hotly against my own. Your breath, sharp with unsweetened Vodka, blowing against my face whenever you turned to speak.

I talked to my girlfriend. She talked to you. You talked to me. The bowl wasn't my first. The comfortable sensation of the marijuana eased my nerves a bit and then seemed to fade away. My legs grew numb. My thoughts grew heavy. My speech slowed, then, simply stopped. Voicing the growing terror was impossible. I was trapped inside my body.

I hadn't even finished my drink. I'd smoked one bowl. I was helpless.

I could feel you pushing closer into me. When you leaned over to kiss me my eyes were wide, my mouth motionless, but you persisted. I guess you didn't want my participation, only my compliance.

My girlfriend left crying. I was alone. And you were still there. Your breath on me. Your thigh against mine. Could you tell that I blacked out? Did it make it better for you — or just easier?

You had me in your room. Your bed was soft and you were hard. The weight of you thrusting me into the down. Each time my certainty renewed that one more push and the bed would swallow me whole. It would save me from you.

Flashes of memory still cut across my psyche: a box; a whip; a mask; a bottle of something cold that burned when it touched me. Only you will ever really know what happened that night... silver linings…

The morning came, full of sunshine and regret. I was hung over, my limbs full of salt and my stomach full of snakes. You were nowhere to be seen. The house was quiet. My chest flooded with a sudden sense of urgency. I threw my legs over the bed's edge and my body followed. My leg muscles were melted rubber but the door was ajar.

You'd left two 20-dollar bills, a pocket knife, and a bag of weed on the carpet by the bed. I palmed the money, grabbed the knife, and opened it before using my arms to pull myself forward, toes scrabbling at the rough carpet.

My fingertips closed on the open door as your shadow fell over me, its weight oppressive against the morning sun. "Hey baby, don't leave so soon. I'm not done with you yet."

The silk in your voice slid down my throat, choking me. When you reached for me I could only think *Not Again.*

You don't know me that well. I never told you about my six years of self-defense training. I never told you I was taught from a young age to never be afraid to protect myself. Or about my dad, who made sure his teenage daughter knew every painful pressure point on the human body.

The knife in my hand moved faster than your fist. Your tight grip on my hair slacked, letting my head sink to the ground before your incoming fist passed through where I had been. My arc had landed the knife deep into your calf just below your knee.

"Bitch!" you shouted at me, more threat than accusation, your foot kicking towards my face. I clung to the handle, your blood slick on my hand. I raked the knife blade down to your ankle, aided by the fierce movement of your foot. I never saw your face after that, but I imagine you were surprised.

You fell back. Blood was everywhere. Blood in my eyes. But the path out was clear. I threw myself through the door and found my way out of the house. Somewhere near the yard, my legs regained themselves and I ran. I ran from you. I ran from that night. I ran from the blood still wet on my hand. I knew if I made it to the woods, I'd be safe again.

I wondered, what did you tell the hospital when you went? What did you tell the ambulance driver who came to get you from your room full of sin?

You wanted a victim. You wanted to take something I couldn't get back. You wanted someone to use without consequence. I wasn't your first, was I? You had practice. You had a routine. But I am not your victim.

I am a Valkyrie and you are weakness personified. I continue to grow. I am strong, happy, fulfilled. I am part of a community. I am whole. My scars have healed. Have yours?

Sincerely,

The Unbroken

Dear Me,

You've certainly done some stupid things in your life, but the decision to put your head in the sand, ignore the risk of prostate cancer, and worry more about the discomfort of having a biopsy than the dire consequences of missing malignancy turns out, in hindsight, to be your dumbest move yet. And it could very well be your undoing. In fact, the odds are pretty high you'll be lucky to live another five years — and have to fight for whatever time you manage to salvage — rather than living twice, or even three times as long, like those actuarial tables suggest a man your age, 74, who is otherwise in good health, might reasonably anticipate.

How can this be? You're married to a physician — a woman recognized for her excellence in medical practice, at that. Your primary care provider is equally skilled. You've known them for 30 years. You practiced with them for half those years. And that's another thing. You're a FUCKING family therapist! You're supposed to know about denial and self-sabotage. And you spent years collaborating with doctors. You know more about disease than most of your mental health colleagues.

Speaking of which, what about the implications of learning you were BRCA positive, that Angelina Jolie gene that puts your daughter at increased risk for ovarian and breast cancer, and you at greater risk for prostate cancer?

Yours is Gleason 8, by the way. You know, the nasty kind. Much more likely to grow quickly and spread. It's working away inside you right now, even as I write this. Does it know that you're planning surgery? Shhhhh! Be quiet, for Christ's sake (actually, for your sake). At best, it's got another 8 weeks — poetic, huh? Gleason 8, and 8 weeks? That's the very soonest a date can be arranged with one of those robots. And that surgeon, young enough to be your kid? Should you request an older colleague, one with more experience? He said you could, but that would squander precious time. Likely take you past the 90-day threshold between biopsy and surgery, after which outcomes are not as good, statistically.

There's another thing. Maybe you should have paid more attention in graduate school to that subject, instead of faking your way through that course. It's all about *statistics*. And it's statistics that helped you dig this black hole for yourself three years ago. When that other urologist told you that you needed a biopsy, and you — and your physician wife — ignored his advice. Why? Because of some bullshit articles in the medical literature that suggested men were being over-tested for prostate cancer, and being subjected to unnecessary procedures as a consequence, and at a financial cost. And the cost of morbidity, when *statistically* the majority of men who reached their golden years would develop prostate cancer but die of something else, it was actually because the majority of them would have the slower-growing kind.

But wait. You have that kind, too. Your prostate is like a little diorama for the disease: two of six lobes exhibiting BPH (that's benign prostate hyperplasia, to the uninitiated), one with Gleason 3+3=6 (no cause for alarm, Mr. Kelly — we recommend "watchful waiting"), one with 4+3=7 (the level at which that other urologist would have been strongly advocating treatment) and — our feature attraction — not one, but **two** 4+4=8. Which, along with your PSA of 10.1 (up from 6, three years ago, and in a new and worrisome bracket, notwithstanding a free PSA of 18.2), suggests — statistically? You are SCREWED.

Actually, after the surgery, you'll be incapable of engaging in that sport.

The good news? You won't want to, after the adjuvant therapy (that's fancy medical lingo for the other stuff they'll be doing to your body when the microscopic metastasis [how's that for alliteration?] they missed wakes up and takes up where Mom and Dad left off when that robot up at the hospital kidnapped them.)

Whew.

Of course, some of this is based on statistics — the

ones in that nomogram (no, that's not misspelled) they plug all your numbers into. The mathematical marvel that, based on your personal numbers, estimates the probability of your CSS (cancer specific survival) at 10 years as 98%. So, what are you worried about, Man? Why the melodrama?

The Devil's in the details, Bro. Read the fine print, Fool.

Significant probability of undetected metastasis to the lymph nodes (that's the Interstate system that will ultimately take your little pioneers to the bone and that, my friend, will wipe the smile off your face). Hey, there's always the possibility you'll be in the 15% who are a surgical cure. That's like winning the Mega Millions Lottery. The second prize is nothing to turn your nose up at either. One or two positive nodes out of twenty buys more time than three or more. If your Gleason score was 7 vs. 8, even more time. Afraid that train has left the station, Pal? What to do? Well, it's been less than one month since the biopsy, and less than two weeks since the diagnosis. Only days since the follow up X-ray, bone, and CT scans.

The good news is that you may qualify to dance with that robot — and the Devil — *if* your heart is healthy enough. It'll be like watching two officials scrutinize the monitor after a questionable call. The anxiety of waiting to learn whether they'll rule in your team's favor or for those other bastards. That's the ticket. Think of yourself as a team on the bubble. You barely made it into the big dance and managed to survive your first elimination game. You're looking for an unlikely upset. You're praying for the Final Four. Take a deep breath. Maybe this nightmare is some bazaar mutation of March Madness rather than a cruel April Fool's joke.

If only that were the case!

Yours Truly,

Frank Kelly (aka, your *other* self)

VOLUME III

Dear Cookie Dough,

We need to talk. I can't believe I'm saying this, but... it's time we moved on, went our separate ways, and forgot we ever happened this season. The thing is, it's almost summer, and even though you've been so beloved and mouthwatering to me these past few months, you can't just latch onto me and expect me to be okay with it, you know? To be honest, you're just way too clingy (in all the wrong places, I might mention), so I need you to escort yourself out of my life and my kitchen ASAP.

You're great and all, don't get me wrong. We've had some sweet times: Christmas, or the whole holiday season, if we're being honest with ourselves; Valentine's Day, when you were smothered in five kinds of chocolate, ooh la la; and all those Saturdays where the sole fact that it was the weekend was a good enough excuse for us to get together for a little midnight rendezvous where I could indulge in your gratifying presence.

I mean, how could any sane person resist your suave texture? The creamy peaks and waves of rich velvet bliss, the subtle crunches of chocolatey undertones, the edible paradise that melts on your tongue, and the saccharine granules that grip your taste buds and caress them like a lover's kiss? Oh, tantalizing Lothario-dessert, you overpower my senses and leave me breathless.

Despite your irresistible and seductive ways, our relationship is unhealthy — quite frankly, my heart has been put through a lot because of you, beating to an unsteady rhythm when you're near — and I need to stop letting you control me so much. I'd like to think I'm strong when it comes to refusing your temptations, although you're so addictive and enchanting that I'll probably send you a "thank you" card when I'm diagnosed with heart disease or diabetes in a few years. You're just *that* dangerously sweet, Sugar.

Please, don't take this parting personally. We're bound to meet each other again someday, especially when my appetite is stronger than my will to resist you. Hey, if it makes you feel any better, I always liked you better than brownies.

-Your Ex-Devourer

To Whom It May Concern,

This letter is to express commendation for one of your employees at store #065472, located on 52nd Street between 5th and 6th Avenues in Midtown Manhattan, NYC.

The employee — "Hannah" — was kind, gracious, and altogether accommodating during my recent visit into your clothing store. I was looking to buy a new pair of jeans and, perhaps, some slacks, as it had been many months, and even years, since I'd last purchased any wardrobe items for the bottom half of my body. Moreover, I am used to enduring these often dis-comforting shopping experiences with a young woman by my side — one with whom I would have been roman-tically entangled, to be more specific — but as the situa-tion currently stands, I am alone.

Hannah saw me eyeing the khaki- and navy-colored pants and asked if I needed any assistance. I replied, "Do you mean with the pants or with my life?" And together we shared a hearty and jovial chuckle over my remark.

Recovering quickly, albeit with a bit of blush painted upon her cheeks, she said, "Let's start with the pants, and work from there." Maybe she even winked — I can't recall. But I think she might have winked.

She helped me find my size in both length and waist, then led me over to the changing area and asked her co-worker, "Donnie," if he could set me up in a room. (Incidentally, I found Donnie to be the most bored and lackadaisical employee, with one eye on the wall clock and another on his handheld gaming system — and yet, I come to praise an employee of store #065472, not to bury one, so let this be the end of my Donnie-centric commentary).

As I was being led away to change (my pants, I mean), I shot a glance at your dear Hannah that could only be registered in the key of *longing*. Without a moment's hesitation, Hannah picked up on my silent cue and inquired, "Would you like me to stick around and help you decide if they look alright?"

"Would you?" I replied, "Oh, that would be most appreciated." Truly, in that moment, I felt that love and life seemed possible once more.

Do you happen to know if Hannah is dating anyone? I didn't see a ring. Just wondering.

With Hannah's expert assistance, I ended up purchasing two pairs of Rugged Steel-Toe Boot-Cut Jeans, a pair of Stone Washed Five-Pocket Relaxed-Fit Jeans, and two pairs of the Pleat-Less Thin-Hip-Fit Everyday-Work Slacks, in navy blue and camel tan. I also took Hannah's advice and purchased several of your Wrinkle-Free No-Dry Button-Down Oxford Shirts, on sale for $49.50 each, and was able to take advantage of the Buy-One/Get-One sale on Business Belts as well. I am hoping that Hannah receives the commission for these purchases, and if there's someone I need to speak with to ensure that it be so, I insist that you let me know.

In conclusion, I do wish to extend my compliments to your very lovely employee, for her professionalism, as well as for the way her green eyes, combined with that Corvette-red lipstick, left themselves implanted in my mind and in my heart, all these many days hence.

Sincerely,

Josh Lefkowitz

P.S. Again, in all seriousness, do you know if she is dating anyone?

VOLUME III

To the Dutch Girl in a Summer Dress,

Years ago, when I was young and backpacking through Europe, I saw you across the street in Amsterdam.

You walked hurriedly on the sidewalk, and your flowing dress trailed behind you in the wind. In my memory, you are wearing a bright red dress and the space around you is nearly black and white.

You hastily glanced at your watch and in an almost continuous motion, you stepped to the curb and put your hand out as if to hail a taxi.

But you didn't stop a taxi.

With hand outstretched you nearly stepped in front of a passing bicyclist. In a brief, wordless exchange (at least it was a mute conversation from where I stood way beyond earshot), you convinced him of the importance of your unknown (to me) agenda and the speed at which you had to make it happen. I always thought it was a job interview and you were running late. I don't know if you even gave him a chance to accept the mission or if you just invited yourself to jump onto the back of his bike where the bags are usually strapped.

He continued on with you as his cargo.

I assumed you both laughed and carried on, maybe even falling in love a little until you were at your stop, just a couple of blocks up. I don't remember how far you traveled, and in writing this to you now, I wonder if it was even far enough to justify stopping a stranger to have them cart you along at all. I always wondered if, in fact, you both felt bubbling love.

Did you exchange numbers? If you didn't, is this missed connection ad something he should've written a long time ago?

Where are you both now?

Are you happy?

It's funny because this memory feels more like a waking dream. I'm unsure if you ever existed, which is okay; I don't to you. But with the amount of weed and caffeine that coursed through my system that day and the days before and after, I can't be sure. Except I am sure that you're a character that has taken residence in my mind, reliving that moment of hailing a bicycling stranger, the two of you falling in love, and then, parting forever over and over again.

Anyway, if you do get this, do write me back. Hope all is well.

LETTERS NEVER MEANT TO BE READ

Ta,

-Amol

VOLUME III

To Wonder Woman,

You walk around, wise beyond your years. Naive only because I've kept you sheltered.

But you've been through more than the average girl.

You're not the average, posh pink princess.

What was it that Hippolyta said? "They don't deserve you."

She was right. They don't.

He doesn't.

Not even I deserve you, but I have enough sense to recognize that when God gives you a gift, it's better to accept it and treasure it than toss it away into the world, like so much garbage.

And so, I guard you, protect you. But I haven't always been able to, despite my best efforts. And even now, I'm conflicted. Eighteen does not mark a magical anything. Overnight, one does not become an adult.

Maturity comes through adversity and perseverance. You've done that. You continue to do that. Have faith. You'll make it through.

VOLUME III

So tonight, you asked for another crumb. Another piece. Still trying to make sense of a story, and person, that will never make sense. You don't want to give up.

With your lasso, you compelled me. Always wanting the truth, not knowing that this mere morsel was always inside you. Our memories are always there. And so, I helped you retrieve it.

What a wicked, hurtful tale it was. Eight years between it and us, and still it burns.

It was when there were but four of us, soon to be five. He was continents away. He couldn't hurt us from there — or so I thought. And we had just moved. I remember that townhome well. It was probably my favorite out of all of them. Two stories, with the light gray carpet. Straight up the stairs, into the master bedroom that overlooked the back. I remember the light would stream in, just so, because I never once put up curtains. The bathroom was huge, with a walk-in closet just on the other side. There wasn't a loft, but a little ledge of sorts, so that if I was up top, and you were downstairs, I could look over and see you without effort.

And there we were, downstairs, when it happened. I was running around, tending to the baby, my feet gliding back and forth over both tile and carpet, as I ran from the laundry room near the garage to the living room and back. And as I was tidying, you came running, with a lacy red bra in hand. A bra I had never set eyes on before. All lace and underwire, well worn.

LETTERS NEVER MEANT TO BE READ

"Where did you get this?" I remember asking, as I couldn't fathom where it had come from. I owned nothing even similar. And while I was standing, mouth agape, in the living room, here you came again. This time with a satiny blue one, with cups just my size — whereas the red one was too small.

And so, I followed you, out of curiosity as much as shock, to a black book bag that had sat by the door for several weeks, as I didn't want to put it back in the garage. And out you pulled another. And another.

All four bras, none mine, were different sizes. Different bands, with different cups. Four different bras. Four different people.

I was shocked.

And there I knelt, looking through the rest of the bag's contents, making sure there weren't still more. My mind running, but no answer becoming clear to me.

I can't for the life of me, even now, think to why I bought all the lies, and not just about the bras. And that particular story he gave me? It wasn't even a good one.

I remember being on pins and needles the rest of the morning, waiting on that call. The one that was made almost daily, from half a world away. And I was trying to be calm, to be rational, not accusatory. But remembering even now makes my stomach knot.

VOLUME III

I remember giving him a heads up, that we were about to have one of "those" talks. A serious one. And I wanted answers. Truthful ones this time.

But it never mattered what I wanted. Not then, and certainly not now. Those lies rolled off his tongue like water over an umbrella. Just as easy as you please. The lyrics, "Can't touch this!" come to mind.

And I bought it. Bought all of it. Like the fool I was — but am no longer. I bought it. And to make matters worse, I stayed. We all stayed.

We stayed through that. And through the next round. And the next round.

But after three plus strikes, the gloves came off. Still it wasn't me who left. He walked out. To do number three the same way he'd done numbers two and one, I suppose.

So tonight, as your golden lasso is wrapped around me, and your eyes staring wide at my words, I can see recollection dawning. A memory awakened. Retrieved. The truth in my words, chipping away at the lies. And you knew. You so easily saw what it took me years to see.

He was in the wrong.

-Grace

Dear Gram,

I've begun to build a life that I hope would make you proud. This country house that is like yours, these relationships, this baby on the way, my ambition, my pen, my self-worth... all a reflection of your good deeds. Thirty-five years ago, you welcomed a baby into your home and took care of a colicky fuss the way only a grandma could. I have so many fond memories from my childhood that include your laugh, your cooking, and your strange quirks. Teenagers make babies and get divorces just as fast, but you were there with your warmth, your grit, and your know-how.

I remember your bustling house as an anchor to so many lives. The foster children, your children, and your grandchildren. After we moved out, it was a destination, a place just down the road to get a tasty treat or play in the old barn. A place for peace and quiet, a place for loud birthdays and horseshoes, a place for barking dogs and sweet lemonade.

How did you know my nature before I did? How could you tell where my inner demons and shining appetite would take me? I have come full circle, but you always wanted to be a writer, wanted someone in the family to be a writer. You had those mail-away programs that you likely saw on TV. You showed them to me — I even participated a time or two — but like everyone else, I was haphazard and careless with time.

I often wonder what you would think of my stories now? What would you think of my letters, the publication, the gossip, the feud? You would probably submit ten letters at a time. You would likely demand to see the proof copy of each volume before it was released. We would have long conversations about story ideas and murder plots. You would likely press me on deadlines and word count. Is that what you are doing now? Is that you there, pushing me along, keeping me to task?

I remember going with you to Catholic Church and watching your eyes. I remember you teaching me about personal hygiene and the importance of deodorant on a hot summer evening. That wooden half-door between the kitchen and living room and its creaky springs, your plain but oh so satisfying way of cooking, your dogs, your cigarettes, and the way you made me feel. Me, Dad, and Uncle cutting wood for the winter, your calls from the door, your strange sayings.

You could walk a cat down the road with no leash. You trained little dogs to hate everyone else in the world, but adore you and Grandpa. You could make dinner with nothing in the fridge yet feed ten people. Oh, if I had your budgeting skills. There is no telling what you could have done for those in need with my income. No, I'm not rolling in it or anything, but things seem to come up, frivolous fancies that you only heard about. You were no-nonsense in some regards, yet all nonsense in others.

I wish I knew more about your childhood, about your life. I get bits and pieces but not everybody wants to talk, and Grandpa moved on. I'm glad he did, he is a good man. You were an orphan, and out on your own at the age of twelve or thirteen. I don't really know what life was like with my biological grandfather, but I know he wasn't that good to you and the three kids you had with him. My oldest aunt knows, but she's in another world...

I've always been interested in finding out what kind of genes you gave us. Your look, those eastern European features and smile, are all dominant traits that everyone shares. I want to do one of those DNA tests where you mail away a sample, but I can never decide which one and I'm not so sure if they are at all accurate. I often wonder if you took one, could you find some long-lost sibling or figure out where your ancestors were from?

You would love my wife. She has a lot of your caring qualities and has been used to having less. "She's a looker" is how *you* would describe her for sure, but I have no doubt that you two would get along. She takes care of the elderly that have memory issues, a thankless job for those families that don't seem to want to remember either. She gives me a hard time but has a good heart, and I know she is going to make a wonderful mother.

Your death was sudden, and I wasn't happy with the explanation or the outcome. Seems to me that medicine prescribed caused your death, but nobody can bring you back. I said something nice and thoughtful at your wake, but I wished we all could have gotten along better and danced instead.

I showed up there in my cleaned and pressed Army uniform. I thought you would have liked that and I really didn't have a suit at the time. I was just getting started, and now I seem to have come full circle once again. Something that I thought would have made you so proud is about to end. I have some big decisions to make, but these all seem to be less about me as time goes on. I know you would support me, but it's hard to know what to do all the same.

How do you like all the letters I've published? So many more are coming out soon. I used to have to beg people to send in letters, now they come by the bushel. I also dedicated my first book to you. A dirty crime novella is not the greatest work I'll ever do but it's a start, and I know you would have appreciated the gesture.

I hope I am living up to your potential. What I mean by that is that I often wonder if you were coming up during this time, with all these opportunities, what you could have done. Societal expectations, access, and opportunity have all changed so much, even since your death. I just hope that I am taking advantage, and I hope you would be proud.

LETTERS NEVER MEANT TO BE READ

Time just keeps going, we lose ourselves, and we don't even know why.

—Marc

VOLUME III

To Whom It May Concern,

In the event that you are reading this, it means that you are now living in *Her* house. In all likelihood, the walls which hold so many dark secrets have been painted over, as it has happened so many times before. The putrid, odd odor, which has its own presence, has been masked by homemade cookies and freshly varnished wooden floors. Even the estate agent did not disclose any of the strange disappearances of the previous owners.

If that is the case, and it is still light outside, I suggest you get out, and get out now. For you are not alone, and you are not safe in the dark. I used to tell myself I was alone, that there was no one else there each time I switched off the lights. I too believed that what was in the light was in the dark, but that was not true. There is something in the dark hiding from the light. You can hear it come alive late at night, when it is quiet.

At first, you can only hear noises; the house settling in the background, followed by loud erratic breathing which seems to pour in from every corner of the house. The tapping is what makes you doubt that you are alone;

the tapping of bony fingers echoing through the darkness. The kind of tapping that can drive any sane person mad.

Yet, that is not what gets you in the end; it is when everything stops, and the only thing you can hear is your own murmuring heart. That is when you know. She is a hunter, stalking you in the darkness. She has no name, no face, no identity. She is good at hiding; she has been doing it a long time. My advice to you if you do decide to stay is do not trust your own reflection. Good luck and Godspeed.

Regards,

The Previous Owner, Whose Face She Now Wears

Dear Jeff,

You asked and I said yes. I meant every word I ever said to you, but it's clear you didn't. When you left, you took a major part of me with you and I will never be the same. I'd go as far as to say you ruined me because, flash forward 13 years, I'm still hurting. I'm still mourning the loss of you.

When I first saw you, I didn't think much of you. I didn't even look twice. I just thought, "Great, a new supervisor jerk to tell me what to do. He'd better just stay out of my way and I'll do the same." I've never worked well with authority figures or anyone in a position to think they are superior, and you were no exception.

You would just show up to work and go straight to your office. You never tried to interact much, which I thought was a little unusual. I didn't care to get to know you either due to my distaste for upper management. Though, eventually, I did notice you had very kind eyes.

Remember our coworker, Jerry? Well, one day, he came up to me in a rather juvenile way and said all the guys had created a hot and not list. He said I had been voted the hottest girl working at the theater. They were all still in high school and I was an adult so I just ignored him. Jerry also mentioned, after twisting your arm, that you said I was one of the most beautiful girls you'd ever seen.

Somehow, although the situation was silly, it made you seem more interesting. I didn't necessarily care about the thoughts and comments of teenaged boys, but I was curious to know if you really said I was beautiful. After that day, I started noticing you staring at me. You'd shyly look away immediately and I'd just smile to myself.

One night, there was a really nasty snow storm and our manager sent everyone home except you and me. The theater was completely dead and, for the first time, we got to talk. It was one of those rare conversations you get only once in a lifetime that you never want to end. I felt a real connection to you.

From that day on, I began looking forward to seeing you pull up a few minutes late, parking on the sidewalk, carrying some type of fast food bag and drink. I even found myself willingly switching shifts with coworkers just to be on the same shift as you. I looked forward to our little talks and mild flirting.

I finally got up the nerve to ask you about that childish hot or not list. You were so cute and shy, but I was happy you answered honestly. It made me more attracted to you. It made me see you less as the supervisor jerk I wanted to avoid and more as a guy I'd like to get to know more, maybe even outside of work.

One night, I was just about to call my ride to pick me up. You were done counting the drawers and closing up earlier than normal. You offered me a ride home, I hesitated at first, not wanting to make you go out of your way. I eventually accepted and I'm really glad I did.

We were sitting outside of my apartment, laughing and talking; you could cut the sexual tension in the air with a knife. I took a chance and kissed you on your soft, perfect lips. I felt as if I perhaps misread your body language, so I reached for the door handle and tried to make a run for it.

You grabbed my arm, pulled me back into your car and gave me the most passionate kiss of my entire life. It was like a scene from a movie; I felt like I was outside of my own body watching. I felt sparks, fireworks, everything. It was so intense. You parked your car on my sidewalk in your signature way and we made out, tearing at each other's clothes all the way to my front door.

It was like a love scene at first, until we stopped for some reason. Although we had ripped each other's clothes off, we didn't make love. We did stay up all night talking, holding hands with nothing on but a blanket. We talked until the sun came up and I made us pancakes. It was the most intimacy I'd ever shared with anyone.

You confided in me that you had lost everyone you

loved in the span of one year. Your mom died of cancer, your dad, stricken with grief, died shortly after. Your brother disappeared without a trace, your sister-in-law took your niece and moved without warning. Your girl-friend went to California and your Grandma moved to Arizona with her lover.

You showed me a vulnerable side that only attract-ed me to you more. I wanted to be a loved one you could rely on to always be there. Just after that night, I knew I wanted to be your family and your friend forever.

We were inseparable and couldn't keep our hands off each other. This proved difficult, since you were my supervisor. There was a strict, no fraternizing policy at work, but we'd sneak in kisses and hugs whenever we could.

We had both recently gone through break-ups from long-term relationships. When I met you, I knew I never wanted to see my ex again. I'm not sure if you felt the same; you never seemed to be able to give me 100% of yourself. You were still living with your ex's mom, which I found troubling.

You were so afraid to stay the night with me, fear-ing her reaction and being kicked out. I understood that your break-up was abrupt. Your ex moved to California to live with her dad, leaving you behind with nowhere to go. You really should have moved out when she did.

Although we hadn't been dating long, I felt a powerful connection to you, a connection I hadn't felt before and still haven't with anyone since. It took all of my courage to ask you to move in with me, and I was crushed when you said no. I felt that we weren't on the same page for the first time and that you were still holding on to your ex.

I tried to slow things down for you since it was clear we were moving too fast, but fast felt right for me. Things were so hot and heavy up front, I was still there but I felt things fizzle for you. Sure, you were still romantic, you'd send flowers to work, call my sister and find out what my favorite restaurant was, and have food sent to me.

You were the most romantic guy I'd ever dated and it hurt having to hide our growing love at work. It hurt even more that I felt you holding back when I gave you my all. I told you that I wrote poetry very candidly and from the heart. I don't hold back in my writing, I just write how I feel, as I feel it.

You asked if you could read some of my work. I had never let anyone read any of my private poems; it was equivalent, to me, to being naked on a billboard. I hesitated at first, but after we shared a deeply personal, emotional moment together, I felt I could share anything with you.

When your childhood dog got sick and had to be put down, you cried. I held you and cried with you. It was such a beautiful and emotional moment, and I saw flashes of a future with you. I saw us getting married, having kids, traveling the world, and growing old together. I saw forever with you.

We lay in my bed that night, and you didn't jump up to sneak back into your shared home. You rolled over, held my hand and said, "I know this is really sudden, but if I were to ask you to marry me, what would you say?" I said yes, without any shred of hesitation. I was 20 years old and we had only been dating for 5 ½ months, but it felt more than right.

I gave you my stack of poems; the equivalent of me ripping out my heart and placing it in your hands. Days passed. You ignored my calls and you avoided being on the same shift as me at work. It was unlike you not to call and say good morning or good night. I tried to respect your space, but at the same time, I was worried and confused.

I purposely pulled a double shift just so I could catch you. You went out of your way not to speak to me. I saw you standing outside talking to our manager. You handed him your keys and badge, you got back into your car and disappeared down the street; I felt my entire heart shatter.

One of my coworkers walked up to me and handed me back my stack of poems. She said you left them there for me. Knowing how deeply personal my poems were to me and how it took a lot for me to let you read them and the fact that you left them somewhere everyone could read them just added insult to injury.

I was still in shock and disbelief that you quit and didn't say goodbye. I called and texted you numerous times until the number was disconnected. I cried for days, even having to call in sick, missing work and classes. I couldn't get out of bed; all I could do was cry.

Word eventually got out at work that we'd been dating. It was nice to not have to hide anymore, but sad we never really got to celebrate our love publicly. I loved you more than you'll ever know. I sometimes feel like things would have been different if I'd just chased you out to the parking lot and went with you. Wherever the hell you went, I wish I'd gone too.

I realize now that your childhood dog dying and my poems about my ex were the last straw for you. I wish you understood that I loved you, not my ex. Those poems were written in the moment. Two years later, out of the clear blue, I finally received a message from you via Myspace.

"Hi, girl, this is Jeff. I have never used Myspace before but I thought it would be a way to find you. To my surprise I did, so I created an account just to send you a message. It was nice to see a pic of you cuz I haven't seen you forever. I have been wanting to tell you some things for a really long time now and I'm gonna feel so much better getting this off my chest. I want you to know that I'm really sorry for how everything went down with us. I know it was my fault. I feel like I could have done things different. I don't know what you think of me now but I have to tell you that I have been thinking of you ever since. I honestly never meant to stop talking to you completely. I ended up just leaving town for a while to try and figure my life out (I went to Denver by myself, but I didn't get to try the Black-Eyed Pea). I was really confused in my life back then and it hasn't really changed since. I find myself constantly making choices I regret. I don't know where life would have taken us together, but I really wish I had kept you in my life somehow in some way. You are one of my favorite people I have ever met. I just want you to know that you are a very special girl who will make someone very happy someday. I wish I could put into words the impact you made on my life. You may not know it but you helped me through some very tough times and I want to say thanks for that. I learned so much from you by seeing life through your eyes and by your outlook and approach to things. I want you to know that despite my actions, everything I told you I meant. I'm trying my best for this message not to sound like a desperate person trying to get back with you, because that is not the case. I just wanted you to know these things because it has been bottled up for years now. I have always debated just stopping by or looking up your dad's phone number to call you, but I was scared of how you would react. It is such a relief to finally let you know. I hope everything is good in your life and that everyone in your family is in good health. I don't know if you will even give this message any thought or if you will even reply.

But if you do say whatever good or bad, I will at least know that you read this."

I've read this message countless of times but it still leaves me with nothing. I sometimes torture myself by reading this and crying my eyes out. It's been 13 long, hard years for me and I never did get any closure. I responded, but you closed your Myspace account and I never got answers to the thousands of questions I still have. I understand that you were hurting but all you did was pass that hurt onto me. I still cry daily for you; I have not moved on like I should have.

I found out, through a mutual friend, that you got married and had a son. Good for you, I truly am happy for you. I'm glad it was so easy for you to move on. I haven't been so lucky in love. I think I still compare every guy to you.

When I found out that you were married, I'll admit, it hurt all over again. Up until then, I think I had this secret hope that we'd run into each other and the magic would start where we left off. I'd run to you in slow motion, we'd have a whirlwind kiss, and the rest would be history.

I now realize that will never happen and it's time for me to wake up and move on. I hope this letter receives you well because this is the closure I never got. I hope you live a long, happy life. I hope all of your dreams come true. I really wish you well.

VOLUME III

Goodbye,

-Peaches Mothersbaugh

To the Love that Never Gave Back,

This is not just a letter, but a piece of my heart put on paper. A piece of my heart that you took and I'm sure will never give back.

From a tender age, I promised myself I would never give myself to anyone. I kept to myself, often with my nose inside a book or earphones plugged in to drown out the world. But then on that one fateful day, you came into the library and sat in the chair facing mine. Do you remember? I know I do. Slight irritation irked me as I wondered why this stranger had invaded my space.

Then you looked up and caught me staring. Our eyes locked; the deep brown of your irises reminded me of the smell of dirt after the first rains, or the first sight of a cup of coffee early in the morning. You smiled and continued pulling out your books from your backpack. You set a Dan Brown novel on the desk, perhaps it's that moment that won me over.

Or maybe it's the fact that I kept seeing you, every day. That library almost seemed abandoned with barely anyone there to take up space. Yet you chose to sit facing me, always. I would've thought it unsettling had you not been so attractive. It was difficult, but exciting, to think that maybe you were just as attracted to me. Why else would one take up stalker-like tendencies?

It felt as though a kaleidoscope of butterflies had exploded in my stomach the day you finally spoke to me. The smile you shot in my direction, the way your hand grazed my shoulder after we'd exchanged phone numbers and goodbyes. There is no need for me to recount the events to you, I suppose. You know all this. I just want you to realize that the effect you had on me may have been greater than you knew.

Our bond grew as we developed a friendship outside those library walls. Where I normally spent most of my days staring at the pages of a book, I now stared at your face. Your scent became one I longed for in your absence. Your smile shone the way to some of the brightest days of my life. With each day, your affection chipped away at the concrete walls I had built around myself before finally letting them crumble to the ground.

I thought that we were going somewhere. That maybe the emotions aching within me would spew from your mouth, letting me know we were on the same page and a relationship would grow from there. That day I hung out at your house, I thought my moment had finally arrived as we sat there on the couch facing each other. You put your hand over mine and told me I was like the baby sister you never had. Perhaps you saw the tears pooling in my eyes as those of joy, when in reality, I was heartbroken.

How could you say you saw me as a sister? A sibling? I wanted you to be my lover. All those moments when your face would hover close to mine, I wished to close the gap with a kiss. When your hand accidentally brushed my thigh whilst reaching for the gear shift in your car, I wanted you to do more than just touch me. I wanted you to be the Romeo that lived, with me as your Juliet. To make Shakespeare's metaphor 'beast with two backs' come to life. Clearly your thoughts were far from this.

Just when I thought I couldn't be any more incensed, I saw you with her. You told me she went by the name Vivian, but she was a thief in my eyes. She stole you from me. Was it her silky black hair or her long legs that went on for days, or simply the fact that she was better than a short, plump, and boring bookworm? I want to know, really.

The thought has haunted me for nights on end. I imagine you burying your face in her full bosom, planting kisses and running your hands over her sweet caramel-coated flesh. All these thoughts run through my mind whilst I'm alone in my bed, when I really should be with you. I can barely count the number of times I've had to convince myself that it would happen eventually. That you would break up with her and realize that you've loved me all along. But as I write this letter with reddened eyes and quivering hands on a tear-stained piece of paper, I realize that may never happen.

I could settle for a friendship with you, but the pain would chip away at my soul until I am nothing more than a shell of who I used to be. It'd be like sitting in the world's largest library and not being able to touch a single book. Instead, this letter serves as my goodbye to you even though it pains me to say. I wish you all the best in life. Part of me curses you for making me believe that we could ever be in love, the other part thanks you for showing me that I am capable of feeling for something that actually has a pulse.

Maybe one day I will be loved in return.

Yours,

The Girl with a Broken Heart

Dear Woodpecker,

Out of all the houses and all the walls in the entire neighborhood, why'd you have to choose mine? Was it the color of my siding? Did the architecture meet some sort of predetermined woodpecker criteria? Are you just a form of karma come to punish me for calling in "sick" to work that one time?

Mr. Woodpecker (may I call you that?), you are an absolute nuisance, and I think you know this, too. Otherwise, you would kindly cease your obnoxious — and might I add unnecessary — commotion, taking the hint when I pound my fist against the wall or open my window so you can clearly hear my desperate pleas for your hasty departure.

But no, you just keep on peck-peck-pecking away like there's no tomorrow. A plague upon my house, that's what you are, sir. You know the sound those springy door stops in the wall make when they're pulled back, like a giant "boing" where you can almost feel the vibrations pulsing and radiating outwards, and they eventually fade? Well, okay, I guess you wouldn't know since you live outside and everything. And you're a bird.

Anyway, that's what you sound like at six in the morning on the outside of my bedroom wall. Except you're twenty times louder and the clattering noises don't ever fade. Really, your forceful beak has this way of producing an ear-splitting racket resembling that of a sharp, high-speed hammer, or perhaps a nail gun being shot into my wall only a foot away from my head. It's unnerving, to say the least.

Look, I'm sure you have a fantastic personality with the looks to match, and all the other peckers of wood in the forest probably bow their beaks down to your majestic ways like the king that you are. But not me. I'm no peasant of yours, Mr. Woodpecker. Now it's your turn to listen to *me*.

Here's my proposal: Go away.

Simple enough, yeah? I would be glad to assist you in house-hunting for a new abode so you can continue your practices while maddening someone else, someone worthier of your attention. Hey, I heard that the Teagues recently had their siding refurbished; maybe you could go introduce yourself to them? I'm sure they'd be delighted to have you. You'd be helping me out, too, especially since your services would be great payback for Chris blasting his lawn equipment every Saturday at eight in the morning. Killing two birds with one stone, am I right? Oh no, I didn't mean to offend you with that last part, Mr. Woodpecker. But now we're even...

Please, Mr. W, I'll do anything to be rid of your incessant company at dawn. I thought you were supposed to be a woodpecker, not a rooster — learn your species, if I may be so kind to suggest. We can work together in this, can't we? Just leave me be, so I can finally sleep. I'll even forgive the past three months' rent you still owe me.

—Your Former Landlord

VOLUME III

Dear Mom,

I wish you were alive so I could fess up to a lie I told you, years ago. I wake some mornings with the memory of that day gnawing at me, the deception gripping me with sadness and anxiety. This morning's snow flurries, outside my office window, triggered that memory again.

Sixty-eight years ago, a three-day snowstorm dumped two feet of snow on us in Belmont. For three days, us kids had to play in the house, and at times we got loud. Each time, you scolded us with "pipe down," because Cindy was sick in bed again with strep throat. You stressed about it all. Cindy was sick for almost two months. Frequently, Dad had to take time off work from his new job to take her to the doctor. The road in front of our house was eventually plowed, creating a snowbank in front of our yard. The snow had stopped, and I begged you to let me play outside. You said I could, but I had to take Beth Ann and keep her close by. I remember you said, "You can play out there, but you've got to put on your coats and *goulashes*."

Once outside, I went down the street, out of sight,

and took off the galoshes. I was desperate to slide on the snow. Rubber soles don't slip as well as leather soles, so I took off the boots. I was skating on the hard-packed snow in the street when you yelled at me to get my galoshes back on. I knew the snowbank was too high for you to see below my knees, so I yelled back, "I have 'em on, Mom!" You didn't answer, and the door closed. I reluctantly slid back to where I had stashed my boots and put them on.

Beth Ann came over to where I sat in the snow, "You lied to Mom. She's gonna tell Dad, you know."

I latched tight the top buckle. "No, she won't. She can't see over the snow, Sis. Mom's just guessing."

"Well, Mom does know. She knows everything."

I didn't think you could see that I took them off, so I lied to you. I feared Dad would spank me for disobeying you, but he'd also whip me with his belt for lying. So, no matter what, I knew I would get it.

Later, you called us into the house. It was evident you had been crying. You said the doctor had called with Cindy's test results and that the strep throat had advanced into rheumatic fever. The doctor called a prescription to the pharmacist. I was sent to the drugstore since Dad was at work and had the car. I grabbed my hat and coat and ran out the door before you could remind me to put on my galoshes. I knew better... but I knew I could run faster in my shoes than in the dang boots.

LETTERS NEVER MEANT TO BE READ

Running home from the drug store, I slipped on the ice and fell. The bag and bottle slammed into the icy sidewalk. The bottle broke and the antibiotic blended into the ice and slush. Panicked, I ran back to the drugstore. With tears in my eyes, I told the pharmacist what happened. He smiled and said, "No problem," and refilled it at no charge. When I got home, I didn't say what happened. I didn't want you to know and then tell Dad. I figured if he knew that I fell and broke the bottle, it was because I wasn't wearing my galoshes.

When Dad got home, you hunkered into the living room and talked long into the night about Cindy's condition. The doctor had said with rheumatic fever, there would be a risk of heart damage. All night I worried that you might tell Dad about the boots and I would get a thrashing. But nothing was said. The next morning, Dad left for work and said nothing. Nothing was said the next day or ever.

Just recently, Beth Ann and I talked on the phone. We discussed our health and how our bodies are aging. I said, "You know, Sis, the older I get, the more I remember the bad things I did as a kid and with those memories, I have regrets." I told her about the lie still festering.

Beth Ann replied, "You got to let it go, Kevin. Mom knew. She didn't say anything, but she knew. Also, Mom swore me to secrecy. Before you got home from the drug store, the pharmacist called and told her what happened. He also said there would be no cost for the replacement antibiotic. And, he asked her not to scold you 'cause you already felt so bad about breaking the bottle."

I've since learned everyone tells lies. Some are white lies. Some are whoppers. I've said both. Looking back, I regret what I've said and didn't say. Mom, you told me "always tell the truth." I still hear you say that, especially when there is a choice. Truth, or lie?

Each time, I struggle with the decision.

How do I tell you I'm sorry? My words on paper, with this letter?

I feel awful that I lied to you, Mom, but then again, maybe you already knew.

—Kevin

To Our Lost Cheese Puff,

I've always been a cat person, hands down. And as far as cats go, you were a keeper. Just the right mix of spunk and cuddles — a perfect match for our family.

Your soft orange color with the white paws deemed you a creamsicle, no doubt. My oldest came up with the term — and your name.

Cheese Puff.

Our prowling little tabby cat.

And though my opinion of you was high, it was never about me. It was never about you. It was all about... my daughter.

You were a gift. A fur baby blessing. The very best birthday surprise she'd ever had. And she loved you. Truly, she loved you.

We'd talked about how it was a big responsibility to have a pet. It wasn't all cuddles and snuggles and sunshine. It was kitty kibble and Tidy cat litter, all needing to be swept up. It was hairballs on the rug, and vet visits for shots. It was keeping a full water bowl on your mat and cleaning up poop scooped onto the floor. And she did! She rose to the occasion taking care of you. You were like her baby, her little furry baby. But your time with her was short.

For our home sold in record time, and my father? He's highly allergic. So we made arrangements to have a coworker watch after you while we were hours away, moving into a new home and town.

A couple of weeks went by, and my daughter was anxious to see you again. She feared that she might never see you again, and it was hard on her heart.

Shelley sent some pictures of you, coddled in a stranger's arms, obviously purring as they stroked you under your white chinny chin chin. She loved it! She cooed! Oh, how she missed you, Cheese Puff.

She wanted more pictures, so I assured her I'd ask again soon. But weeks turned into months, and I kept failing to make you a priority. Until finally, thanks be to God, we moved out of my parent's home and into our own place again. At which point, one of my first orders of business was to come and get you from Shelley.

I called and left a voicemail, but no return call followed. I tried again later, still nothing. No big deal. But a week or so went by, and I knew my girl was getting antsy, so I texted Shells, and whew, finally, a response. Unfortunately, it wasn't good.

For you, our Puff of Cheese, had obviously craved

adventure — and catnip on the street. And when Shells had opened the door one day, MEOW! Out you ran! And Shelley, in her ridiculous high heels, had been unable to make it down the driveway before you were two blocks away. An orange and white blur, out into traffic. How long ago had this happened, I asked? A day? Two days? But no. At this point, it had been weeks. Weeks since last she saw you.

I hadn't the heart to tell my daughter, so when she asked about you next, I made up my mind. I was going to find your papers.

Thus, in the midst of unpacking, putting away plates and blankets, I stopped what I was doing and began rummaging through file cabinets. The paper with your microchip number had to be somewhere. And towards the bottom of one folder, there it was. Crumpled and torn in the corner, but still there. And I began going down a list of vets and animal shelters, just calling and inquiring about your whereabouts.

It wasn't until about the 11th place that I was told the microchip number I had? It was wrong. The numbers were 9, 10, or 15 numbers. And yours? It was 12. I tried deciphering where exactly you'd been bought — because I mentioned you were a gift, yes? But what I failed to mention was you were a gift from someone who hated me, scorned me. Who was manipulating my daughter, trying to buy her love, so yeah.

I had your papers. But chunks of info were missing.

Blacked out. I had not the name of the shelter, or the address, or day. I was going on so little, but I had to try. I even went to my daughter and asked, did you go with him to get Cheese Puff? And she said... YES! PetsMart in Colorado Springs, hallelujah!

I looked up the address, and make yet another couple of calls. And guess what? They remembered you! Another stroke of luck! Through the blessing of technology, they were able to provide me with the last three numbers on your chip.

One step closer. And the "found" registry, online? You were in it! Yes!

At this point, I'd love to tell you this story has a happy ending, and that you and my oldest have been reunited. But...

I can't. Not yet.

See, the "found" registry was updated in December and it's now March. But don't worry,

I'm not giving up hope. I'm going to keep calling. Because as much as my daughter loves you, I love *her* a heck of a whole lot more. And I'll do anything to have you two reunited. Anything.

Stay strong, Cheese Puff, wherever you are. We're looking.

—Grace

Pat and Will,

This is to inform you that Mom is dead. She died five years ago. The reason I did not tell you before is because she made me promise — and she was very clear, vehement, and adamant about this — not to tell either of you (Pat or Will) that she had died. Her feelings were that if you wanted nothing to do with her when she was alive, then she did not want you to be informed about her death. She made me promise that many, many times. I am not making this up; you can verify this with her sister Ramona — she told her also that she wanted no one to know about her death except Ramona, Rebecca, and Gloria Jean. She wanted no newspaper notices at all. This put me in a very awkward position: do I honor her wishes and keep silent, or do I break the promise I made to her on her death-bed, her one last wish, and tell? I have wrestled and struggled with this dilemma for all these years.

The reason I am telling you now is because I had a long talk with my pastor and he told me to go ahead and break the silence because you deserve to know.

She was cremated, and her remains are in an urn next to Dad's in the niche at the national cemetery in San

Antonio.

I am sending this letter to both of you.

Kindest Regards,

Your Sister

Dear Fountain Hopper,

I was walking by the fountain on Main Street yesterday at 14:00 when I saw you. You know the fountain. It's flat like a chessboard in the ground. You were tall as a tree, smooth skin over muscled shoulders. You wore nothing but tatty striped shorts and a smile. On your head was the most glorious mop of golden curls ever to grace a man's head.

As I walked by, struggling with two bags of vegetables, eggs, and rice, I saw you amongst the spurts of water, climbing higher with each graceful spit. To be clear, the water was spitting, not you.

You twirled around, hopping to a drumbeat that was playing in your head. That beat must have been played by a one-handed drummer with vertigo.

At first, I wanted to smile. There was pure joy in your face, even as your bare feet landed on old cigarette butts with soggy nuggets of burned tobacco sticking to your soles.

However, I changed my mind as you began to whirl, your own free-spirited worship to this urban temple we all live in. As you spun, top-like, wobbly, and out of control, the water flicked in beads from the tips of your curls and created a rather impressive spray.

What was equally impressive, though, I must confess, hideously unwelcome, were the number of drops which landed directly in my eyes and on my lips.

Are you aware that the water used in the fountain is in fact recycled via the drain that borders it? Do you ever sit and watch the number of dogs, children, bicycles, and drunk people that weave their way through that fountain, usually leaving bits of themselves along the way? Bits that recycle back into those frothing wet spires.

Well, I've sat back and watched them, and I can tell you that I didn't appreciate receiving those various leavings in my face.

If you insist on continuing this bizarre ritual of urban worship, then I would like to suggest you shave your hair to spare me and others the free blessings which your golden curls bestow. As beautiful as those curls are.

In closing, dear Fountain Hopper, I'm not telling you to stop doing what you love, because it clearly makes you rapturous. I am merely saying that not everyone benefits from it, so think about who you're anointing next time, and if they've even asked for it.

Don't let that get you down though. I can assure you that your dancing is indeed infectious.

LETTERS NEVER MEANT TO BE READ

With the Loveliest Greetings,

Someone Who Likes to Write and Just Wanted Groceries

VOLUME III

Dear Holy & Stressed Wife,

I beg to apply for sex. I have been feeling horny lately (for over a week now). I don't know the most appropriate time of the day and day of the week to fix it since you are always indisposed. I know Mondays and Tuesdays are not ideal because it's the beginning of the week, Sunday is off because it's a holy day, Thursday and Friday are not too convenient because you would have been fanned out towards the weekend; therefore, I am looking at Wednesday since it's mid-week. I can't say about time; you are usually tired and stressed out in the evenings, too sleepy at night, hurrying in the morning, the afternoon is also too hot, besides, you won't be around in the day. I have considered after dinner but you would be too heavy, too hungry in the morning, feeling hot in the afternoon, so I don't know. However, I want to apply two to three weeks upfront, so that you can fix the day and time that is convenient for you. I promise it would be strictly missionary — no stressful styles, and it would be quick too. Please kindly use your good office as a wife to consider and approve my application.

VOLUME III

Thank you in advance.

Your Husband

Dear James Patterson,

I hate you, sir.

-A.M.

P.S. Perhaps *I hate you* is not good enough to explain my disdain about your general existence. I once looked up to you because of your *Maximum Ride* series.

It was something about how your creativity was unchained to the tethers of normality. You dared to write with a female protagonist. You dared to write stories about characters who could fly. You even wrote about love and romance.

If it weren't for you, I wouldn't have had the exact set of tools to write a story about the God of Love. I also knew how flying could be depicted.

Back to the *I hate you*, as it were. You are a bad person. I like to think that you are trying to get unknown names into the open by doing your "co-authoring" nonsense. No one can write a book and a half per month all year long. You've said in interviews that you give the "co-author" an outline, but from my personal stance, that means… you aren't the author.

I get that this is a bold-faced claim from a nobody. Heck, I can only hope that someday this letter creates tension between us, because I will be that popular.

What is that new thing you're trying now? *Book shots? Booklets? Mini bookies?* The thing where you take your character and put them into a miniature novel? That's called a *short story*. You're trying to make a lot of money from short stories by re-branding them. It's stupid. I don't care how much money you make, I will never acknowledge the things you think are accomplishments.

That brings us to my last reason for my opening remark. Remember the *I hate you* from the start? You went on to ruin my favorite series, doing what all aging writers do. You wrote more about the characters long after their story was dead and wrapped it up nicely. You committed that crime at least six more times. You ruined your own franchises for money. I know it was for money.

You're arrogant and in your own book trailers. You aren't the only author that's done this, but you are the capital felon.

Your integrity is compromised. Your plots are your own but written by someone like me. Someone whose name gets turned microscopic under your huge ego.

But hey, like I said before, I'm just a small-time author, paid for writing letters. You don't have to listen, and you won't. I don't have to buy your books either.

Still, *I hate you.*

Sincerely,

A. M. Flounchell

VOLUME III

Dear People Who Got Rid of Their Little Library,

I am writing to express my intense displeasure at the removal of the Little Library from your front garden wall.

Little Libraries, as you well know, benefit the community by affording all free access to a book-sharing receptacle. I hope you can understand why I, for one, believe that there cannot be too many Little Libraries in the world, or even in our community.

I first discovered your Little Library while I was running a small errand for work. Such was the nature of the discovery that I had not the time to browse the collection of donations therein, and instead made a mental note of the existence of your Little Library with the intention of returning when I had sufficient time to dedicate to said browsing. Imagine my surprise, then, when I, not only with a thirst for discovering hitherto unheard-of books but also with a backpack full of books I wished to donate, returned to the location of my mental note to discover nothing less than that where there had once been a Little Library — a wonderful wooden box filled with worlds infinite — there was now nothing more than a hedgerow.

VOLUME III

As I can only imagine that your deplorable actions mean nothing less than that you are opposed to imagination, I will spare you the task: I was dismayed! Not only is there one fewer Little Library in the world — a crime surely worthy of at least six months' imprisonment — but that which has been removed was the only Little Library for several streets in a considerable radius. What is more, there seems to be no intention of replacement.

I understand the trouble that may befall Little Libraries. I have heard tale of another, one which is dedicated to children's books, which suffered those troubles of being left out at the mercy of the environment. It is truly a terrible shame when a wooden box left in someone's front garden is damaged in any way, and I offer my condolences if that is indeed what happened to your Little Library. The difference between the two instances, however, is that the former conjured up a new wooden box for use as a Little Library and included a note of apology explaining what had happened and the reason for the necessity of a replacement. You, however, have shown no such intention to replace your Little Library.

If you truly do not wish to carry the burden of such an important public service, that too is understandable. In either case, however, I would ask that you either reinstall your Little Library or arrange for the establishment of a new one and notify me personally when and where the new Little Library shall be made available for public use.

LETTERS NEVER MEANT TO BE READ

Yours faithfully,

An Avid Reader

VOLUME III

Mr. Unreliable,

You never realize how important a quality or virtue is until it's lacking in your significant other. Dependability. Reliability. These are characteristics that I took for granted in prior relationships. And now?

Well, let us look at a couple of case studies, shall we?

Tonight, our oldest was away at a friend's house. Their family lives a half hour away from us. We'd set this play date in motion last week and, knowing how much time I was going to have to spend in the car on a Friday with five kids WITHOUT the added trip to pick up our oldest, I asked if you'd be able to get him. You assured me you would.

We were to pick him up by no later than 5, as our friend's daughter had dance class that evening. I asked if that was going to be a problem. You responded that no, it wouldn't be. I was home fixing dinner, about halfway through, with our loud, hangry lot running in and out, and — let me state too, that I'd put a reminder in your phone that tonight was your night to pick him up. *Don't stay late at work, tonight of all nights.* I'd also texted you earlier, just to be sure you remembered, in case you didn't see the reminder. You'd asked me to remind you, and so I did.

Still, it was about 4:20, and you hadn't yet called to tell me you were leaving work, so I called you. You'd let your phone die. Again. And you'd left your phone charger beside the bed. Again.

Consequently, I had no way to contact you.

The minutes rolled by and then it was 4:45.

Again, we were half an hour away, so I was hoping you were already on your way out there, so when the phone rang, I thought it was you. No, it was our son's friend's mom. She knows they live out in the boonies, so she offered to meet me across from our home in town. "Great!" I said. And I hung up and called you to let you know. Still no answer.

Dinner was almost done, all but the vegetables in the skillet. But as everyone was finishing up their steaks and quinoa, I started wiping sticky faces and putting socks and shoes on everyone while prepping them, saying, "You guys, we're going to have to head out to get your brother soon." They reminded me that you are supposed to pick him up. You said you would.

"I know," I said, "but just in case. Just in case."

I got everyone dressed. It was 4:53 and here you came, crossing the threshold.

LETTERS NEVER MEANT TO BE READ

You grabbed a plate and sat down, and I reminded you that you were going to pick up our boy.

"I know," you said. "I will."

I looked at the clock, knowing there had been a change in plans. We were still no closer to the friend's home. What gives? "His mom offered to meet us at McDonalds on their way to dance," I said. "I'm about to head out." It's 4:58.

"Let me finish eating first."

I was confused.

"Yes, well, I have to be there by 5."

"It'll only take a minute to get there," you said.

I ignored your blasé attitude, handed you the baby, turned off the stove, and ran to the bathroom before grabbing my keys.

I don't understand how you didn't see that you were inconveniencing several parties here. Not only were you not making good on your promise to get our child, but you were obviously not concerned about the previously agreed-upon pick-up time. Then, the mom offered to do us a huge favor and meet us closer to home, but she had a prior engagement, too, and so they were in a bit of a rush. But you didn't seem to care about any of that. Or the fact that if we make it a habit of showing up late, they may not invite our son over again. And while I get that this all seemed petty and insignificant, it really was just another straw on the camel's back.

Like when you kept telling me that we needed a butcher block island for the kitchen, needed more space for the dishes, and needed more counter space. Okay, fine. I'll find us a deal on that so we don't spend a fortune clearing up some cabinet space. And I found one. For a super great buy of only $100. And what luck — it matches our cabinets.

I messaged the seller while you were standing there, and yes! Glory be, it was still available. And I checked with you about picking it up and you said, "Well, we've got a lot to do today, let's aim for 3 or 4 p.m."

It was 9 a.m. when I sent the seller the message.

We had almost NOTHING to do that day, aside from cut the grass — which your DAD did. Not you. And so, throughout the day, you brought up a couple of plans that revolved around 3 or 4 in the afternoon, but I gently reminded you that you had agreed to go get this butcher block.

Then 2:30 rolled around and you told me, *sigh* "I need to get a shower. Let's not pick up the butcher block. We need to save money."

What?! With half an hour until pick up?

And not just that, but the seller was supposed to pick up HER boys at 2:30, but because 3 is when we said we could meet, she had asked her husband to pick them up so she could be at the home to let us in to get the island.

I gave you her info, her address, her name, and I said, "Fine, YOU call her and explain."

"Oh, I will," you said. And you wandered to the bathroom.

The shower started.

Ten minutes to 3, you messaged her, saying we couldn't make it. Though I'm embarrassed to think what excuse you may have made.

Knowing you, you used our kids as your excuse, as on so many other occasions.

I get the whole saving money thing, I do. But then right after that, you found an elliptical for sale for $50, and you asked me what I thought, and I said go for it! You messaged the seller, and yes, it was still available, and close by. I waited, and waited, and waited, and finally I asked, "Are you running out to get the elliptical?"

And you said, "Naw, we didn't need it."

"Did you message the seller to let him know?"

"No."

"So why even message him in the first place?"

Then there was the night you were going to pick up the sofa after work, the one that your mom found for us since ours was destroyed. But you piddled around after work, like you normally do, and you ended up getting home well after dark. Your dad pulled his truck around and waited about picking up dinner because he was going to drive you to town, but you came in, dragging your feet, and with only a few minutes to spare before pick-up time, again you made an excuse. This time, it was that *you're tired*. It's always something with you. Always.

You told me that during your first marriage you would cut the grass every weekend. I find that hard to believe, despite you raving about how much you love yard work.

You're always talking about putting out plants, and planting shrubs, and I just roll my eyes and ignore you. You were in that home in Ringgold for how long? Two years? And the entire time we were together, I can count on one hand the number of times you cut the grass.

Whew!

In fact, it was so bad when we started seeing each other that the grass out back was knee high. A huge branch had fallen and was taking up half the yard, and every weekend you would tell me you were going to cut it. Week after week after week. That was autumn.

When spring arrived, I was honestly so tired of looking at that branch, and the knee-high grass that hadn't been cut in SEVERAL seasons, and the leaves all over the front from last fall, that I called someone to come cut it.

In less than two hours, the yard looked fantastic. Curb appeal had returned.

Your unreliability is so bad, in fact, that if you say you ARE going to do something, I just mentally check the "Nope, never gonna happen" box and move on.

Like the chore charts. I've been hearing for over a year that you're going to make some chore charts and, really? There is NO excuse.

I bought the dry erase board. But then you said you wanted to take it to work to have lines put on it. For rows. Columns. Stickers. Never happened.

I even put the board IN YOUR CAR and you never even moved it from the front seat. What was up with that?

Then I made printouts that I was going to put up for chores, but no, you didn't want me to do that until you laminated them. Again, those pictures are still matte and have been moved back into the house more than once.

Canceling the auto policy when we got a better deal?

Applying for the million and one jobs you had saved to Indeed.com when you quit your job?

Getting money from the bank?

Paying the electric bill? Yes, the one that was shut off THREE TIMES in one year — not because you didn't have the money, but because you straight FORGOT.

Need I go on? Because I can.

I love you, I do. But, Baby, please. For the sake of everyone involved, you've got to start following through. It would mean the world to me. Think on it.

With all my love,

-Grace

Dear Sir,

You think you're special, don't you? One of a kind. Unique. Well, newsflash, Sunshine, you're not and you never were nor will you ever be. Different, yes, but not of an exclusive breed to the rest of us. The most impressive thing about you is your intelligence and even that is almost shadowed by your overinflated ego.

You hide behind this mask of perfection. You can't do wrong. No, not you. You who are so *perfect* it blinds others to what kind of person you truly are. Intelligence, looks, social skills... The list of what others deem perfect or outstanding goes on for a long time. It's just a pity the only thing on this list that's even remotely perfect is your mind.

Yes, you have looks, but there are more attractive people out there. Yes, you have all these friends and acquaintances and you can communicate with people you don't like without the cold civility many of us have, but you seem so unaware of the fact that some will hear the things you've said about them. The slimy, nasty things you don't have the guts to say to people's faces.

VOLUME III

In fact, this is where your perfect mask is shattered into a million pieces, exposing the kind of person you truly are.

You're not a perfect person (and if you were, I'd trust you less). No, what you are is a slimy snake who thinks himself above everyone else. You're convinced that you're so superior and it comes out in the way you talk, so subtle no one would notice unless they're looking for it. Your snide comments are like your venom. Everyone thinks so highly of you so if you've said something bad about them it *must* be true. Because there are those of us who apparently never do any work and constantly slack off, creating more work for those around us. Because we're apparently leeches that are just there to feed off the end result.

Yes, I never do anything at all. Not once did I assist a friend of mine. No, he merely did everything himself. Of course, I drag him down because I'm obviously a lazy and selfish brat. I just stand there and look like I'm doing something when it's really him doing all the work.

Once upon a time, I might've believed that to be true. After all, I was a person who admired you at a point. You, who have achieved things I could only hope to barely succeed at. You used to be the sort of person I aspired to be like and someone I hated hearing stupid rumors about.

Then I got a reality check. As my world turned darker and the detriment in my mind grew, I lost many of the illusions impressed upon me. I stopped looking at the good side of people. It was then that I realized what you are.

You're nothing more than an egotistical, narcissistic bastard who talks to everyone like they're inferior or a child that understands nothing. You always have been and I don't think you will ever change. You're a selfish coward who would rather tear someone down from afar rather than do it before them because you can't imagine the consequences if it goes wrong for you.

All the teachers idolize you too which helps no one. You're the perfect student — one who always gets the best mark you can possibly achieve, one who always asks questions that delight them no matter how irrelevant to the matter at hand...

I loathe every fiber of your being and hope you rot in the deepest pits of hell.

Yours faithfully,

— Anonymous

VOLUME III

Dear Parents,

I never intended to come out to you in the way that I did. And for that, I apologize. I had it all worked out in my head. I was going to sit down with you both and explain to you that the woman you met was not what you believed she was to me, and that I was, in reality, gay. I wanted to do it calmly, and I had this dream that you would be able to work through it and come to terms with a gay son, and that I would be able to really be myself around you without having to be careful to keep what is a fundamental part of who I am, completely silent.

Sadly, that was not to be. She became pregnant, and you summoned me to the house, demanding to know what I planned to do. You refused to accept my answers until I finally blurted out that I wasn't going to marry her because she was already married.

I stopped listening after the first few minutes of your yelling, until you called me an abomination. At that point, I figured, how much worse could it get? I took a deep breath and yelled right back at you, "Do I need to remind you that it's a relationship with her AND her husband?"

Then you did exactly what I feared you would do my entire teenage life. You told me to get out and never come back. Well, to be fair, you did amend that to say I could come back when I could lead a straight and moral life in your eyes, and in the eyes of God.

I ran out the door, emotionally damaged goods. I threw up a spray of gravel in my haste to leave, though I didn't make it very far before I was blinded by the tears streaming down my face. I sat in my car alternating between anger and sadness. Then, when I was too numb to feel anything, the little voice in my head asked when you became so self-righteous that you carried the eyes of God in your pocket, and I knew I would be all right as I started to laugh, albeit with a soft tinge of hysteria.

I think I mourned for you then. I realized that I would never again be able to look at you as authority figures. There would never again be a time when I would be able to feel safe or protected with you. I don't know any other way to put it other than that, as parents, I realized you had ceased to exist, even though you still lived.

I thought, maybe, I was overreacting. That is, until I started receiving phone calls from the family that you called, telling them about me. There is nothing quite like receiving threats of physical harm from your brother, and being told that you are not welcome with any part of your extended family.

Eventually, we did start speaking again, though the damage done to my relationship with my brother and extended family appears to be irreparable. In a twist of irony, another member of the extended family came out, and he was accepted warmly. I know you know who I'm talking about. After all, you have a better relationship with him than you do with me. Then again, I can't imagine that when he came out to you, you invited him to burn in hell, either.

I want you to know something important. It is incredibly painful that I cannot share my life with you. I have been with my partner for twenty-three years. You denied me the ability to call you when we were having problems. You denied me the ability to call you and share in the good times. You only know half a person.

What do you think things would have been, if the circumstances of my coming out had been different? I don't need an answer, not anymore.

Sincerely,

The Son You Didn't Want

VOLUME III

Dear Dandelion,

Hello. I hope you've been well. I would have started with "good morning," but I'm not in the habit of lying, as you know.

I've noticed that you're distancing yourself from me. Moved out of town suddenly, haven't responded or reached out to me, new car, transferred schools. By the way, do your scholarships transfer with you? You live on your own now; new pet too, I heard. A grizzly German shepherd, retired service dog.

Here's the thing. I haven't seen you since Raymond and the hospital. I haven't talked to you since the airport. If it weren't for your counselor, I wouldn't even know you're still alive. Your dad thought that you committed suicide and I helped you.

I don't have a problem with you moving away. I don't have a problem with you getting a new dog and not introducing me. I have a problem with you ignoring me, ignoring your sister, ignoring your dad, ignoring everyone from home.

We're not on the same page. We are not going

through the same things. We miss Raymond too. We need you too. We love you too.

We're most definitely not in the same pain, but we're in pain too.

The pain never goes away, and we never forget that pain. We grow stronger and we value them more. It will always be painful, but it won't always hurt.

Your Best Friend — if not Girlfriend,

Your Petulant Pansy

Dear Former Fetus,

Hello, Child, Daughter, Son, toaster. I will never get the chance to love you, and there's nothing I can do to change that. I won't be around for you, but I can tell you how to be around for yourself. One day you'll find this when you're hopeless, tired, insecure, and hurting, and there will be nothing left of me but pieces of tattooed tree slices for you to find comfort in.

All I can give you are my letters. And I know you'll either hate them or cherish them, but when you're crying and questioning, you'll hold on to what you can — what you have. You, my friend, are so heartbroken that you're now invested in reading this seemingly personalized message. I don't know what kind of human you are growing up to be, but I just know that you're mine. I will always be your mother, but you will always have yourself. This is Heartbreak 101, from your biological mom.

These pieces of paper will disintegrate by the time you're old enough to read and truly love, but I have hope you'll somehow learn from me, in some way.

Now, maybe you have just freshly severed your

emotional connection to someone, or you're going to lose someone in the near future and you're preparing yourself for it, or you're simply sad you've never been in real love.

Maybe you're wondering why I didn't say *break-up*. I'll get back to that.

There are many reasons for why you might identify as *hopelessly heartbroken*. It's a choice to call yourself that. You decide if your heart has been broken and shattered into a million pieces, or if it has simply been misused or mistaken.

A heartbreak doesn't have to be pain from a breakup or a romantic love. My first heartbreak wasn't a boy — it was my mom. Your grandmother, whom I love very dearly.

Maybe you're thinking you can't live without that person; that they're the reason you're alive, or reason you're happy. It might help to remind you that you were birthed into this wild, wild, world, all alone, and you learned on your own; you survived, lived, and existed all by yourself until you decided to look for more — for someone else. You were perfectly a whole person before you made that decision. You are a perfectly whole person — maybe a sad person — after making that decision. Love and life are two different things (hence *love life* rather than *lovelife*). Even if you lose love, you still have life.

LETTERS NEVER MEANT TO BE READ

Breakups, deaths, arguments, depressing epiphanies — they all suck. They feel like crap, they make you feel like crap, they make you feel like everyone is crap. They're just moments. Sometimes they're long moments, but they're still moments — temporary.

No, you're never going to forget Bella, you're never going to forget Grandpa, and you're never going to forget Fido. You will never forget them because you truly loved them. At least once in our lives, we hurt the people we love, whether we mean to or not. That pain is necessary. That pain tells you that love was real. If your "love" doesn't hurt, it isn't real.

Your heart will be broken. Every now and then, someone will take your heart because you offered it, and it will hit the hard, unforgiving ground with a satisfying crack, and it'll shatter into the million pieces you're used to saying. Then, to be even more rude, they'll leave for you to clean up their mess. Being the human you are, I know you will do it. You are going to pick up every piece of your broken heart because you are proud. It has been tricked, played with, abused, and broken, but at the end of every day, it still works.

It hurts to pick up the pieces. It really does. You're going to cut yourself every time you pick up a piece because of the sharp edges. You're going to bleed and hurt and cry the whole time you're picking up the pieces, but you'll carry on because you remember the happiness you used to have because of this poor little heart.

VOLUME III

A million pieces is a lot of pieces. And it's very hard to pick up every single one. Each time your heart gets destroyed, you lose a few pieces here and there. To when you put the pieces together, there are some parts missing. That doesn't mean it's a broken heart. The holes just mean your heart is more open now.

Mosaics consist of broken shards of glass and tile. Kintsugi is the method of mending broken pottery with pure gold. They are beautiful works of art.

And somehow, so are you.

Sincerely,

Sorry

Dear Jack,

There was never a day of my life that I felt safe with you. Not a night of sleep, or a time of play, when it felt like I had a father who loved, cherished, and cared about me. You stole any sense of purity or innocence that we all should have had, and you made childhood into the most perverse and debased experience.

As a child, you don't really have a choice of whether you are going to deal with the environment you are born into. But as soon as I did have a choice when I turned 18, I made it. And then 4 years later, I made another choice, and that was to expose what you did to whoever would listen. It cost me greatly, and still does to this day.

On my high school graduation day, you made it loud and clear how much you did not value me when you showed up at my graduation, dirty, unshowered, unshaven, smoking, standing in the back of the auditorium in your smug self and without any pride. I was horrified and embarrassed. I have never forgotten it. You are the most selfish person I have ever known, and now you are at the end of your life, and yet you still cannot bring yourself to the point where you actually do the hard thing, and the only thing honorable that is left for you to do. Own your crap!

You will likely make your exit, in the same selfish manner, leaving all of us to live with what you have done, without apology or ownership. What a sad ending to what could and should have been a marvelous life.

Do you know what you have missed? Has it been worth the price? Was it worth the few moments of pleasure each time, to sacrifice the innocence of children who looked to you to be the leader and the light and the protector of all the cruelty that the world offers? For you maybe, but for us? No way in hell!

Here's what you missed:

- You missed my life.

- You haven't celebrated any birthday I have had since I was 18.

- You missed knowing my heart, and it's a great one!

- You missed knowing my best friend and protector and the most loyal, amazing man —my husband.

- You missed the most valuable fruit of who I am and that is my daughters. Do you know what it's like to have to explain to your children why they can never meet or know their grandfather?

Do you know what it's like to have to explain to them repeatedly, starting before they could even talk, and help them understand how unsafe people, especially family, can be? And then to also live, hoping you have accounted for all the potential dangers that exist, praying they will never live through what you have lived through?

● You have missed every birthday of my children, every Christmas, every Thanksgiving, and every Easter dress that framed their sweetness and innocence.

● You missed their high school and college graduations.

● You have missed the fact you have a great grandson that actually looks a lot like you. How wonderful he is.

● You have missed my girls' accomplishments, displays of their talents, gifts, and overall greatness as young women. They are both amazingly gifted, beautiful, wonderful souls, with caring and giving hearts, and so much more which you will never know.

● You missed the pride of watching them win enormous scholarships at high school graduation and the achievements both had in college.

● You missed celebrating the 4 degrees that I hold, and all the achievements with them, the over $80k in scholarships I received when that was not even as common, and the success of my research that has had worldwide impact in other research.

- You have missed feeling the vast pride that is a gift of being a parent and all the surprises that parenthood provides when you have raised your kids with all the blood, sweat, and tears it takes to love, nurture, and protect them from people like you, and yet make them productive and contributing people in an evil world.

- You have missed knowing how successful I am now in my career.

Every day has been a chance for you to make right all the things you have done to those you should have loved and protected. You sacrificed your family, your reputation, and your life for pleasure. You knew better. You know how I understand that? People only hide what they do when they know it's wrong. You had all the rest of society to hold up the standard of what is right.

If I had the ability, you would spend your last days in prison, which is where you belong. I can't even believe you are still alive, but I know it has been the mercy of God. I have spent many days praying you would wake up, you would repent, you would make things right before you're gone. But even God has placed limits on Himself and still leaves the choice to you whether you will do so.

LETTERS NEVER MEANT TO BE READ

As long as you have breath, you can make a choice. But the days and hours and minutes and seconds left on that are running out. What will you do? How dare you take a coward's way out?

— The daughter you never knew

VOLUME III

Dear Dad,

Now that it's too late, I hold a better understanding of you in my heart. Maturity has gifted me with knowledge of the struggles and prejudice you faced in the time when you were raised. My own personal struggles have little compassion for what you endured. As a teen-ager, I learned it wasn't easy for you, that you had it rough. *Well so what?* I thought. Didn't I have it rough with you not being around? Didn't I have it rough with an angry father when you visited?

What I couldn't comprehend back then was that it must have been terrible. All the expectations of a first-born son in a family full of machismo and tradition. All the weight of a first generation American, with skin too brown, who was punished by teachers for speaking the Spanish you learned at home. I understood prejudice was wrong, but I couldn't comprehend how deep that sort of hate can settle into your bones and become a belief that you would never amount to anything. I couldn't comprehend your own mother saying you were too dark-skinned for my blue-eyed, fair-skinned mom. Too brown for this woman you loved. That must have hurt.

Back then, we didn't talk about drinking as a disease, we talked about deadbeat dads. We didn't talk about addiction as a reaction to depression or as a way to self-medicate. Instead, I was taught that your drinking was your fault because you were bad. Now I understand how alcoholism can take over your life and numb your heart. I understand that you drank that much to forget the pain. I learned this only after experiencing depression and my own unhealthy relationship with alcohol. However, back then, I couldn't grasp that the pain you went through was even more hurtful than the violence I encountered. Because, for me, the violence eventually stopped. I was able to leave it in the past. For you, the prejudice was always there. Despite your success, you were still always another, a minority whose parents were from somewhere else.

If I could travel back in time, I would ask if we could talk about it. I would ask for you to explain to me the reasons why you were so angry and unhappy. I would ask why you didn't love me, because that is what I perceived.

If I could send you this letter, I would encourage you to find ways to restart the hopes and dreams that must have been inside you as a little boy. I would ask you to remember how you felt before the world told you that you were wrong. Most importantly, I would tell you that I loved you and that I forgave you for leaving. When I signed the letter "With love," I would know deep in my heart that I meant it. If you were still here, I would rewrite your story in my head. I would accept that you showed me love the only way you could, and I would thank you for that.

Con Amor,

Su Hija

VOLUME III

My Dearest,

I don't believe in angels and I know you didn't either, so I'll spare the dramatic watching over me bit. Instead, I will be honest. It's almost been a year and I'm still as infuriated, shocked, and heartbroken as I was the day I found out. I tried not to be mad at you for leaving, because I know depression was never your fault or anyone else's — but I couldn't. I tried not to let my life fall apart. I tried not to let my hurt ruin my relationships with others. I tried not to let myself down — but I couldn't.

It would be selfish and egotistical for me to dare believe that anything I or anyone else could have said would have saved you at that point. Without indication, you did what you had planned and released yourself from suffering. And, being honest again, I hated you for it. That never stopped me, however. It didn't stop me from feeling intense amounts of pain that I had never previously had to experience. It didn't stop me from constantly visiting your grave those first few months, aching to see you, to feel close to you. It didn't stop me from remembering you. It certainly didn't stop me from missing you. And more importantly, it didn't stop me from loving you.

I absolutely wish that I had known how much you were hurting. I wish I could have helped you. When people mourn the loss of someone they love, it's hard not to focus on guilt weighing down. Guilt and regrets seem to compose half, if not more, of the mourning process, a process that I wrongfully assumed I could will away through partying or find false happiness to rush through. I know now that there is no rushing through, and that pure happiness is a beautiful gift not experienced by all.

I know now that even when I get mad all over again, I don't hate you. I don't blame you. And I'm sorry. Also, **thank you**. I will always wish you were here, but you are not, and it changed me. I've learned how to be more independent, how to value my worth. I've learned that even at the worst moments of my life, I can shoulder through and still survive. I've learned who should be in my life and who shouldn't. I've learned not to settle for anything less than being happy. I miss you as much as I always have, but please know that I have found some measure of peace. You may be gone, but I refuse to let you be forgotten.

I hope to see you again but know that I might not, in the same way that you will not see this letter.

Regardless,

I love you. I miss you. And I'm trying.

To the Goldfish,

They say that every trip around the tank is a new adventure. For the goldfish, it might be a blast. But what about the other fish it has to share a tank with, hm? And what about its mate?

What if, say, a goldfish, married an undersea elephant? And an elephant never forgets. Ever think about how awful it would be on the elephant? Because, see, the elephant feels like she's going crazy. But the goldfish denies there's a problem.

That trip to the grocery store? Never happened. You've got receipts? A bank account showing the trip? Psh. Never happened.

Here comes the goldfish, into the undersea castle, wanting the remote. Leaves the castle, swims almost to the TV, then bloop. Back again. Where's the remote?

But then the elephant puts the phone on the table, goes to the bathroom, comes back, and the phone is gone. There are only two people in the house. The goldfish and the pachyderm. So, where's the phone, goldfish?

I don't know. Never seen it. If you're implying it was never there, there are only so many options. Do you see where I'm going with this? Either the phone was never on the table, or it was. And if it was, where is it now? Because if it was never on the table, we have a bigger problem.

Blame it on the elephant though. Goldfish always do.

Well was Goldfish doing something while you were talking to him? No, yes, maybe? Be more specific.

Was Goldfish on his phone? Was Goldfish eating? Was Goldfish chewing gum? Did Goldfish have a drink in his hand? Was the TV on? Was he walking- er, swimming — ANYWHERE?

Okay then. If any of the above were taking place when you were talking to Goldfish, Mr. Fish is not to be held responsible for hearing your conversation.

Oh, the two of you were sitting on the sofa together, and your hand was on his knee, and you were looking into each other's eyes as you spoke some very heartfelt words, words that had the ability to impact the entire rest of the relationship and where the two of you were going from there? Really? But was that more than a week ago? Yes? Okay. That explains it.

Because while an elephant never forgets, you can't expect a goldfish to be an elephant, or remember that he's seen that tank decor at least a dozen other times.

LETTERS NEVER MEANT TO BE READ

Look, a treasure chest!

-The Elephant

VOLUME III

Dear Richie,

I moved to a new city during my junior year in high school. I didn't really know anyone other than my relatives. The nearest place to go was a big grocery store down the street, along with the fast-food restaurants. My oldest cousin came to visit me one day and thought it would be nice to take me out to get to know the area and the neighbor she knew a couple blocks away. I had to walk, that was cool, but the weather wasn't. It was summer, high 90's, phew was I roasting.

I must have been around 16 years old. What a fine, petite, young, athletic, and fit girl, too. Yeah, I was turning heads by these perverted older men in their 30's and even younger teens that were learning to jerk off. They were all whistling and making awkward sounds, trying to catch my attention. Ha! That was funny, and I could hear my cousin laughing as we walked by. I paid no mind.

At last, I heard another sound, *strange*, I thought. Where is it coming from? I went searching for it, keeping in mind those men hollering earlier who were waiting for an audience. Oh, how they oohed and aahed as I approached. I wasn't heading towards them, but I found *you.*

You were what I saw, and I just had to have you. I looked around to see if you were with anyone, and you weren't.

I spent time with you that day and got to know you. You became cuter and cuter and charmed me. I even took you with my cousin and I to the friendly neighbor. I guess it was weird for me to bring a stranger to a stranger's house, huh? I didn't care. I was into you and they also enjoyed your company. The day grew late, so I had to part ways with you at the location where we met.

The next day, you found me out and about, and I thought *No... that can't be him.* You ran towards me, happy and cheerful, all the way into my arms. I'm glad you did; I hadn't felt that way in a while since I moved. We spent the whole day together at the park until the sun started to go down. It was the weekend and the park was down the street with a clear view from my family's home window. My mom didn't care that I had gone to the park, but she didn't see you come with me. I had an allowance on me and there was a food-bar set up at the park. It was a soccer park but was also used for recreational sports and picnics.

I decided I was taking you home. We snuck in through the front door, down the hallway, and into my bedroom. Good thing I had my own bedroom and had stopped sharing with my younger brother with a bunk bed. After all, I was a growing young lady.

You were amazing… didn't make a peep or my family would have heard you and kicked you out. We played together, and you tried to rub up on me with a smile on your face. I didn't mind so much but nudged you off when you got aggressive. You would give me this look as if confused as to why I did that, even after I brought you home. Did bringing you home mean that you could do what you wanted? No, it didn't.

You didn't like that and started to fuss loudly. I thought you understood. The noise you made was so loud my brothers heard it and came to my room to find us. *Shit! I'm in trouble if my mom finds out from them.*

Soon after, Mom came home before you left, and she saw. She wasn't very happy to see you and questioned why you were there. She demanded to know where I met you and insisted that you leave. My brothers didn't say a word but just sat there and listened to my mom nagging. Of course, you didn't make a sound after all your fussing earlier. You even looked confused.

Suddenly, you got up and walked towards my mom and jumped on her. We were all shocked and my mom screamed. You started to kiss and lick her face. My mom's angry face turned into a smile. You gently nibbled her fingers and she fell in love with you. Everyone fell in love with you.

The time we spent together was less than a year. I wish my mom didn't give you away. I miss you and think about you often.

Love,

Dean

Dear Fear,

Countless times I thought I needed you in order to feel alive. As a kid I was numb toward life. My parents were drug addicts, so I felt better that way. When I started to grow up and develop feelings, I was not a fan. I blocked out everything except you. I was scared to go to school, but also feared home.

Contact with anyone felt dreadful to me, and I thought I might crack. Then again, if I didn't have contact, I'd feel lost at sea. I feared boyfriends staying and leaving. Staying would mean I'd have to lie and hide my home life, leaving would prove to me that I wasn't good enough. I never wanted anyone to feel my burden. Then, adulthood brought on a whole new level of fear. I couldn't make the mistakes and hide behind excuses anymore. I simply didn't have the time and energy between a career, my health, friendships, lovers, and life in general.

One day I realized that you weren't as important to me anymore. I was opening up different emotions and I finally understood that everyone has a past and hardships. I finally realized that there is a place in my heart and mind for every feeling and every sensation. If I allow them to, they intertwine and work together. You are like a broom and just sweep away, never truly cleaning. I've added new tools and learned other ways to clean my life. I do things now that I'd never have allowed myself to do before. You are always there, but now I can step past you. Even though my life today requires more thought into how I live, it's a lot less complicated than trying to find ways to hide behind you.

Gestapo Man

It was an hour before closing at the SPCA, and you strolled in with your long brown hair tied tightly back in a ponytail that flowed down to your hips. An older woman accompanied you inside.

I gave you the usual "Hi, how's it going? How can I help you?" bit. You shouted some gibberish at everyone, and no one understood what you had said. At first, I thought perhaps my ears were just broken because it had been a long day after all.

I chuckled a little and asked, "What was that?" You repeated yourself, still gibberish. It was at this point I realized that you were either foreign, crazy, or both. I shrugged and said, "Sorry, I can't understand you." I went off to start taking care of the animals for the night and my supervisor came over to assist you. You suddenly spoke English and mentioned you were interested in one of our dogs, a pug mix named Sonny. You went to go see him in the back while your lady friend stayed up front to fill out an application.

As I was getting food ready for the dogs, I heard

you in the kennels saying, "Rudy! Rude, sit! Rudy, lie down!" *Who the hell is Rudy?* I wondered. Did you sneak a dog inside somehow without us noticing? Maybe it was a child? I went back to investigate. I opened the door to the kennels and saw you sitting inside the kennel with Sonny. Quick side note: going into the kennels with the dogs is a huge no no at our SPCA. It is dangerous for several reasons. There are signs about it posted everywhere.

I had to approach you about this. "Excuse me," I say as I walk toward you, "You're not supposed to be in the kennels with the dogs, so I'm going to have to ask you to get out of there."

You were quick to respond with, "Well, why does it matter, if I'm taking him home?" This question stumped me for two reasons. One, you didn't know if you were taking the dog home or not; that's not how the process works. Two, I didn't expect you to be such a douche. I had to think quickly. "There are signs all over." I pointed to them on every kennel. "They all say do not enter the kennels. So please get out."

You stood up slowly and then repeated yourself loudly. "Why does it matter, if I'm taking the dog home?" You began to make me nervous, but I couldn't let you know that.

I stuttered a little but managed to say, "Those are the rules." And I motioned for you to exit.

LETTERS NEVER MEANT TO BE READ

You said goodbye to "Rudy" and began to leave the kennel area, and as you did you said more gibberish. Trying to stay professional, I chuckled and said, "I'm sorry, what was that?"

Your voice, even louder this time, said, "Oh, that's right. I forgot you don't speak American. So I guess I'll just have to speak in English for you."

I blinked at you a few times and motioned you toward the front desk. "I'm right behind you," I said as we walked through two doors which you attempted to slam in my face.

You stormed up to the front desk and shouted at my two coworkers, "You've got a real Gestapo back there, don't you?" Honestly, I didn't know what that word meant at the time. High school history has failed me yet again. All I know was that it was meant to be insulting, so I had to respond.

"Are you talking about me? I'm a Gestapo?" We held eye contact for a few seconds.

"Yeah, you are," you finally said, "And I said it in English for you, so you would understand."

"Well thank you very much," I said as rudely as possible and stomped away. I was livid and still didn't know what Gestapo meant.

I heard you shouting at my timid coworker. I stayed out of sight but listened in case she needed help. "How am I supposed to know?" you shouted. "You told me how to get back to the kennel area, but you never said I couldn't go into the kennel!" My coworker mentioned the signs on the kennels. "Let me ask you a question," you said calmly yet frustrated, "How many signs do you actually read?"

My coworker paused for a second to think. "In an unfamiliar place? All of them," she replied. You continued your banter until she had to walk away.

I came back to the front office and my supervisor told me you wanted to walk Sonny. So I got his leash out and sent you off on your walk with him. This was when I told my supervisor about what had happened in the kennels. She Googled Gestapo for me, and I honestly thought it was quite amusing. You called me a Nazi because I asked you to get out of a dog kennel. It was clear to us that not only were you crazy, but you were also childish.

You returned from your walk and I tried to take the leash from you, so I could put Sonny back in his kennel. You threw the leash on the ground just to watch me pick it back up. I couldn't let you have that satisfaction. I laughed and made a joke about you having butter fingers. I put Sonny back and returned to the front desk area, eagerly awaiting my supervisor's response to your behavior.

She took a deep breath, met you at the counter, and slammed her hands down in a way that demanded everyone's attention. "I'm not going to adopt to you," she said.

You immediately became defensive and hostile, but she spoke over you anyway, "You were extremely rude to my staff. You called her a Gestapo?!" You turned to look at me. Your old lady companion said you were speaking Native American and continued to argue. Seconds later we had one of our humane officers escort you out of the shelter.

You're a psycho and a douche, Gestapo man. But I am not mad at you. We talk about you from time to time in the office and your insults are now a running joke amongst the staff. I'm sure you will be happy to know that Sonny was adopted a week later to a very nice older gentleman who is nothing like you.

Your favorite Gestapo,

VOLUME III

Dear New Book Idea,

I hear you. No, really, I do. But I can't get to you right this minu—

Will you *please* stop interrupting me for at least five minutes?

Yes, you are shiny, beautiful, and new. I get that. But I've made a commitment. And working on you now would be like cheating on th—

Could you *please* stop interrupting me?

Now, like I was saying. I'm a married man. I've made a commitment to the book I'm writing now. To have and to hold and all that. And I'm simply not interested in—

Yes, of course you're pretty. That's not the point. I made a promise and—

sigh

Okay. Think of it this way. When I finally have time to start working on you, how would it feel if I dropped you when a newer, shinier book idea came along? Not great, right?

VOLUME III

See? It's not you, it's me. I made a promise to this book, and I'm going to keep it. When our relationship has run its course, you will be first in line. Promise.

Sincerely,

Ditrie Marie Bowie

Charlesa,

I'm sorry I didn't make it in to see you after cancer wrapped its tendrils around your brain. I wouldn't have wanted to see the gray fog of death glaze over your irises and take you away. Cancer is a formidable foe, and I will never blame you for losing.

A lot has happened since you left my world. I graduated from college with my English degree, just like you thought I would. I visited a foreign country. I got married to the love of my life. She has a beautiful 14k white gold ring with a heart-shaped diamond. If you look, you might recognize the diamond.

Remember nine years ago, when I was worried that I would have a terrible Valentine's Day? That was during my phase of going to ask every girl in my class to go out (they all said no).

You were looking through some pieces for your booth in the Antique Mall. Most of the stuff was porcelain, old books, and costume jewelry. Upon hearing my story, you gave me a piece of costume jewelry, and you said something I'll never forget.

135

"Give this to a girl when you know you love her." Of course, instead of taking that ring and giving it to the girl I loved, I took it to 8th grade. It didn't take me long to get the ring confiscated and held hostage in a box in the principal's office. Grandma came to get me from school, and she took the ring.

"Where did you get this?" she asked me. I explained that you gave it to me. My grandma cleaned it, tested it, and put the ring in a box. Next time the three of us were in the same room, she mentioned that the diamond in the ring was real, but you said you didn't give it to me because it was fake. You gave it to me because you loved me.

It took a week for the ring to get lost in the thick of my grandma's collection of items. Eventually the shop closed, you moved on, Grandma moved on, but I didn't forget about the ring. Years later, when I was working at Zales, I realized that I hadn't seen a diamond like the one in the ring you gave me.

Even when traveling salesmen came, I didn't see that shape. It wasn't salesmen that kept the ring in my mind, but rather people buying their own rings. The rings they acquired were brand new, shiny memories, but I had something more. I had something you had given me.

I met Grace in a fiction writing class, but what happened was beyond unbelievable. My first words to her were, "It's not Pokémon Leaf Green. Clearly, it's Emerald." You believe that? I was a snot-nosed punk, fresh off a bad break-up, and a girl took interest in Pokémon, and that's how I responded? I bet you would have liked her. She's sweet, kind, empathetic, and beautiful.

I proposed in the nerdiest way possible. We went for a picnic to the lake, read an entire *Goosebumps* book, and I got down on one knee on the other side of the lake as the sun was setting. I almost dropped the ring in the water. She said yes, obviously. Sometimes when I'm lying in bed with my wife, I see her ring, a diamond newly set in white gold, and I think of how you gave me an heirloom.

At the time, you may not have been thinking about giving me something for a wedding ring, I think you were giving me something you knew would be important. So when I see the ring, I'm sad. I'm never sad to the point I cry, but rather, I'm sad that you didn't get to share in the experience. You didn't get to meet Grace.

I know you'll never see this letter. Even as I write this, tears are popping in my eyes. I just want you to know that I love you. Thank you for believing in me, for seeing what others never saw. Thank you for the hope, and for the little piece of your heart. I'll tell my kids this story someday, for you.

Grace loves the ring,

A. M. Flounchell

VOLUME III

Dear Discount Store Shoppers,

First, to why I am shopping at a (gasp) discount store. I just got my taxes done, and I owe big time. I stopped here to buy something to cheer myself up. For the next few months, I'll be shopping only sales and using coupons. When I asked my accountant about my retirement account balance, he said that I better start saving more. I suppose I'll be wearing flour sack house dresses and live in a trailer home so I can still afford my Botox treatments when I'm of retirement age. Who knew that alimony was taxable income?

Anyway, don't you hate to wait in lines this long? I don't know why they don't have more registers open, especially on a 30% off all merchandise in the Accessories department day. I saw a Michael Kors knock-off clutch that I might consider (I had to pass on the real thing) in my reduced circumstances. I'm sure none of you recognized it from his runway show photos, so never mind — I'll get over not buying it today.

Oh, yippee — now our cashier needs to change the cash register tape. Can't the staff check that sort of thing before they open each day? If that girl didn't have five-inch acrylic talons for nails, she'd be able to change that tape a lot faster.

Miss white polyester jacket, though I am also pleased that Spring has finally sprung, did you not check the calendar before you dressed today? It is APRIL 16 — on my calendar, Memorial Day is not until the end of May. One does NOT simply wear white before the holiday (where I'll be able to get my summer wardrobe at sale prices). And, come on... polyester? That's so lower middle class! If you must wear a jacket this season, try linen. Sure, it'll need ironing, and dry cleaning, but you'll love the way it looks on you. You're welcome.

Mrs. Crocs with socks (yes, I mean YOU), are you unable to tie your own shoes? Okay, maybe you just stopped in to buy your darling granddaughter that hideous top you're holding after a morning of gardening. Do you not want her to have any play dates in preschool? Get a clue, Grandma! And yes, your mom jeans are now back in style, but I can see by the Jordache label on your behind that they've been languishing in your closet for some 30 years. Maybe it's time for an update, don't ya think, hmmm?

Do you all smell something like lamb's wool? It's akin to wet dog, but with a hint of lanolin? Ahh, yes, it's YOU, crochet clothing lady. Your colorful poncho is damp from this morning's shower, and the fiber reeks. Do you ever think that granny squares make you look frumpy? I do. And it's overkill with your crochet bag and jaunty hat. Sure, boho chic is all the rage in some circles, but you look more hobo than boho. I'm sorry if that hurts your feelings; I'm sure you derive a lot of satisfaction in your lonely life from creating your own clothing.

And finally, directly in front of me, Miss Ombre Hair. Your makeup is frightening; I bet you learned how to contour by watching YouTube videos. In case you didn't know, it's April, six months until Halloween. Please do us all a favor and go to Sephora or Ulta and learn how to apply foundation without a spackling knife. Your ripped jeans need to go into the trash — they are more rips than denim. And for God's sake, put on some underwear.

I saw some cute panties in the Juniors department when I was checking out the clearance merchandise. You may think I'm being harsh, but let me tell you, you'll never snag an upper-income husband in the rags that you're wearing. Sure, you have a fabulous figure NOW, but after you get your premenopausal love handles, your Prince Charming will be shopping at his office for your replacement in the wife department. I know what I'm talking about.

Now look at me, alone, in my 40s, with nothing to look forward to other than a microwaved Lean Cuisine and Netflix. Consider yourself warned.

I have been told that I'm a bit of a fashionista, and I want you to know that all of my comments are made with the best of intentions. I hope you all have a blessed day.

VOLUME III

Lots of love,

Karen

Dear Dan,

What on Earth would make you tell Larry, the CEO of Red Tree Inc., that you and I had an evening tryst that spring of 1988 in Las Vegas? I mean, I vividly remember you, the local branch office manager, with the slick hair and heavy cologne, shaking my hand and commenting on my sharp business suit and high heels. I also remember you taking me AND my co-worker Brad to a steak dinner at Caesars. We chatted, or should I say *you* bragged and boasted of your fabulous home, your incredible pool, your fancy car, etc. while Brad and I were simply happy to have a nice steak dinner. We were both extremely tired from a day of auditing the loan paperwork at your branch office, and we were anxious to get back to The Sands Hotel.

As I recall, quite vividly, you dropped me and Brad off at the Sands and we each retreated to our separate hotel rooms, happy to put on our comfortable clothes and relax and watch some TV.

However, back at the corporate home office in St. Paul, an entirely different rendition of that evening was somehow "leaked" to our CEO, Larry. This is how I came to learn of my alleged sordid encounter with you, Dan. My manager Sally, a rough around the edges type corporate controller, called me into her office. As I was an internal auditor, Sally and I had worked together very closely and had even socialized occasionally. She liked to smoke in her office as was apropos at the time and that afternoon, through the haze of her smoky office, she asked me if anything inappropriate happened in Vegas between me and you, Dan. I WAS SHOCKED. Why was Sally asking me this and how did she hear it and by the way…NOTHING EVER HAPPENED!!!

I told Sally about our dinner, which included my coworker Brad, and about the ending of the night, which was just that, an ending. Brad and I had said our good-byes at the entrance of the hotel, and that was that. But my manager persisted to question if it was possible that you, Dan, came by the hotel later and picked me up or came to my room. Sally told me she had talked with Brad, who thought that it was possible that you and I met up after you dropped us off at the hotel. What??? NO!!!

Who else heard about this? I asked anxiously. Sally replied that it was Larry, our CEO, who had come to her with this "news." You see, Dan, I know that you and Larry were very tight. But what would possess you to fabricate such a story with a young 23-year-old woman who had everything to lose? Did it feed your sick, pathetic ego? Did it make you feel powerful, virile, in control?

Did you ever once think about how I might feel or be portrayed? Did it even faze you to outright lie?

During this same time, I was dating a personal injury lawyer to whom I recounted your fabricated tale, and I asked him what I could do about it. Nothing. That is what David said. Just do nothing. There is nothing you can do. It will blow over.

Well, Dan, it didn't blow over for me, not then and not even now. A few weeks after our alleged rendezvous, Abdul in HR told me that he was going to promote Brad instead of me to the senior auditor position. He added that he couldn't tell me the reason because it "might hurt my feelings." I think I figured it out for myself. In my mind I now had only one choice... leave Red Tree and find another job. And I did just that.

But I will never forget you, Dan. I sometimes wonder *where you are now?* Maybe you have since been accused of sexual harassment since the #METOO movement. Maybe you have a nice wife and family and have changed your sick ways. Or, maybe you have been promoted to a big corporate position because you "know how to play the game." You were such an asshole!

But I would be remiss if I didn't say "thank you" as well, Dan. Thank you for giving me this story to tell my own daughter who is now the same age as I was when you tarnished my reputation with an outright lie. Thank you for letting my daughter know that she has a voice and that she needs to use it.

VOLUME III

Sincerely,

To the Eye that Doesn't See,

Most of us are blessed with two eyes, but not you. One of your baby blues has always been as useless as that famous clown fish's lucky fin.

The world can be cruel when faced with an anomaly such as yourself, so I'm sure you had a difficult childhood — I won't deny it or downplay it. But it's not our circumstances, or the cards we were dealt that define us. It's our choices.

Even now, you can't see as you should — despite countless surgeries, but at this point, you need to own it. Acceptance is key.

First it was to correct an eye that faced your nose, then it was to fix the overcorrection of said eye. Then it was cataracts in college — which did nothing for your popularity, or self-esteem, when you had to miss so much school that year. And they've since returned, again and again, in that same eye. So sometimes fate graces you with clearer vision, for a time, but always fleetingly short.

God has been looking out for you — you yourself admit it. And how could you deny that, even for a second? If survival of the fittest held any stock at all, life would have swallowed you whole at birth. At four pounds, one ounce, weak and sick, you entered the world — your mother feared she'd never even get the chance to bring you home. But just shy of your first birthday, she did!

Still, you were always in your sister's shadow — and I'm not just talking about in terms of vision and you know it. What kills me is you deny it — denial.

Denial is your poison. Your go to. Your crutch. And should anyone suggest that you're being hurtful, unkind, or immature, you project blame and shame on them, and oh! The anger! It burns!

Thanks to being babied and coddled all those years following your rough start, and yes, it's still largely in part due to that eye, you developed an unhealthy amount of learned helplessness. It's to the point that, even today, you feel obligated to call for help rather than do anything, and I do mean anything, alone.

It's not that you're not capable — perhaps you are. But we'll never know, because you won't allow yourself to step out. Productive criticism has you coil up and strike, much like the snake that says "Don't Tread on Me." Nothing you ever do is fallible. You're perfect. The bee's knees. Or so you keep believing and proclaiming... outwardly. Inside? You're cowardly. Afraid to face the truth. Afraid to own your failures. Plagued by both real and imaginary insecurities. A several decades-old infant.

LETTERS NEVER MEANT TO BE READ

If I try to hold a real discussion with you, have a heart-to-heart talk, you can't take it. You start saying, "Stop, stop, STOP!" And you hold up your hand, and your voice starts climbing octaves. And I'm faced with two options.

Accommodate your request. Or, keep trying to reason with you. Calmly. Softly. And keep talking. Then the vein in your neck begins to bulge, if I choose to try the latter, and in a very melodramatic, high-pitched tone, you'll refer to me in the royal we and say, "Is this how *we're* going to get our way? Keep talking over me?"

Seriously? Who does that?

I'm usually so shocked at your utter rudeness and immaturity. I'll just stop right there. And then my heart will sink. Because I know I can't win. You won't let me. Ever.

Even frivolous, unimportant banter about the weather, or where to eat, turns into a verbal altercation with you. You'll ask my opinion, but why even bother? You've decided before even inquiring about my tastes as to where we'll be going and what we'll be doing next. And everything I say is just wrong. You tell me so.

You're so superior. How can I ever measure up to your greatness?

They say the eyes are a gateway into the soul. I guess it's fitting then, you only have one. One eye, one way. Like a road in Atlanta. No turnabouts.

VOLUME III

-Grace

*Dear High School
Class of '78 Counselor*

When I was seventeen and complained I didn't know what I wanted to be in life, your answer was, "Why don't you just go be a secretary?" I wanted to tell you then as I do now, forty years later — *Fuck you*. How dare you take so little time with someone attempting to answer one of life's biggest questions? Sure, I wasn't an honors student, but even in 1978 there were more choices for women than teacher, nurse, secretary, or mother. There is nothing wrong with these professions — but there is something wrong with having to select them by default.

I didn't take your advice. I went on to college and as I struggled, I heard your words casting doubts in my confidence as to whether or not I belonged. I earned a bachelor's and eventually a master's degree. I became a manager in charge of people, programs, and a budget. With each new success, your words still echoed in my head and I had to wonder, how much human potential was lost to the world by dismissive words such as yours?

I became a career counselor at a community college. Not because of you, but in spite of you. I wanted to ensure that no one was ever limited by such flippant

151

words again. Everyone should have the opportunity to take stock of their talents and find ways to gift them to the world while earning a living. Not just the boys and the honors students. Everyone should be able to rely on experts to help them plan a realistic path of how to accomplish that dream. That means people regardless of age, color, national origin, citizenship status, physical or mental disability, race, religion, creed, gender, sex, sexual orientation, gender identity and/or expression, genetic information, marital status, or status with regard to public assistance. Even if you don't believe they have a snowball's chance in hell of making it. For in my experience, some do. That means one must have an open mind in order to give advice.

Maybe you quit your job after I left. I hope you did. If you weren't excited about helping young people, you had no right to be there. Just as you have no right to be in my mind for the rest of my life.

Sincerely,

Proved You Wrong and Glad of It

Dear Random A-Hole,

Let's set the record straight. You came into my place of business to rent a home from me, right? You came in with your wife and your parents, I assume so *they* could foot the bill. At the time, I had a particularly nice double wide for rent, and I thought I'd show it to you, even though it wasn't done. I was doing you a favor. I believe it is called being nice, which is a concept that I learned you had no grasp of, despite you being an adult.

I brought Travis along, a maintenance guy who carries a gun. Know why? Because you were packing some serious heat. The gun you barely had obscured looked to be a hand-cannon, capable of killing a bear in a single shot. Outside of that, you had fun tracks going up and down your arms. You donate a lot of blood?

Travis and I did our best to hang back, and just let the four of you converse about the home. You took issue with more things than expected, but I wasn't going to complain. You were the first people to set foot into that home after the eviction of the previous resident, and I had already explained that point to you.

It wasn't until we were all leaving when you said your first words. "Dad, you carrying your gun?" Your father was visually taken aback, but he answered.

"Yeah," he said. That was it. That was our whole encounter from my perspective.

About three days later, I got a call from the Regional Manager. She explained that she got a call from a belligerent person saying that Travis and I had upset him.

"How?" I asked.

I guess *donating blood* had caused you to become so woozy that you thought we were commenting on how nice your wife's butt was. You also seemed to have thought that you told us to stop and we continued to do it. That was when you threatened to shoot and kill us because you were so mad. I told her it didn't happen, because it didn't.

If you had threatened to shoot Travis, it would not have gone well. He's such a red-blooded American that he would have put a bullet in you just for looking that way. That, and I'm not known for objectifying women, sorry. My Regional Manager found it easy enough to believe me.

I heard much later that you showed up at a different property my company manages, and you acted the exact same way. You need a free ride? Some rent taken off your bill when you move in? Think it'll help you do drugs — I mean *donate blood?* Probably won't see you again, but I just want to tell you, nice try.

Sincerely,

A. M. Hounchell

(Former) Assistant Property Manager

P.S. Your wife's butt wasn't that nice.

VOLUME III

Dear Financial Aid Office,

I was never lucky enough to receive your help, but you were like a free money leprechaun that everyone at my college spoke of. Free money, book deferrals, and refunds, but I never saw you myself.

My family wasn't poor, but we weren't rich either. Grants were out of the question. Let me say that again, *I never received a grant from you.* No money for school, books, or anything else when you were passing out $100 bills. I did, however, take out a two-thousand-dollar loan once a few years back and I just finished paying that off. It was the first loan I had ever taken out for college. I spoke to a woman in financial planning a few years ago who said I was on a financial aid plan due to my current academic standing with the college (it wasn't good). But I never cared about that. I didn't get financial aid.

Before we continue, a brief history of my college education is in order. It was bad. I wasn't a bad student and I'm certainly not stupid. I just never took college seriously my first few semesters. My GPA at the time of taking out this loan was 1.9. Yeah, I know.

Let's fast forward a few months into that semester. I had just started dating my husband, moved in with him, and gotten a new job. I wasn't taking my classes seriously (again). So, I decided to withdraw from the college. That way, I wouldn't further damage my GPA, if that was possible. Yeah, I took a hit with the loan, but that was okay, and I still believe it was the best choice at the time.

I took about two years off from school and decided to go back in the Spring of 2017. I paid for four semesters out of pocket because I didn't want to take out another loan, and since I wasn't 25, I was still considered a dependent of my parents. This meant no leprechaun money. With a little bit of overtime, very strict spending habits, and a lot of help from my then fiancé, I was able to pay for college on my own.

After we got married, I was no longer considered a dependent of my parents. Finally, some luck! I completed my financial aid information online, and it asked about my income for 2015 (a financial shit-storm for me). There was no doubt that I was going to qualify for a grant of some kind. I was so happy that all my hard work would be rewarded with a small break. I sent in all my information and anxiously awaited a response.

About a week later, I got a letter from the college saying that I had "exhausted my financial aid." What? You mean the loan I took out and paid off, or the six-thousand dollars I gave you on a silver platter? I marched down to the college as quickly as possible to speak to someone about this letter. The short version of the story is, I spoke to a lady who said something along the lines of: "You were on a financial aid plan back in 2014, and you didn't follow the plan, so you can no longer receive financial aid of any kind (including grants and loans) through the college." I thanked the woman for her help and cried all the way back to my car.

Yeah, I was a shit student four years ago, and I understand why I no longer qualify. But, I took out a loan once, one time. Not to mention, I'm a great student now. My GPA went from 1.9 to a 3.0. Doesn't that count for something? Like I said, I understand why, but maybe it's time you rewrite the rules a little to help students like me. People who really messed up in the past but are now making it work and doing better deserve a second chance.

I'm glad I was able to graduate. I never have to spend another dime there.

-Meghan

VOLUME III

Dear Attorney,

I heard your ad on the radio from a Christian station. You were faith-based, so I thought I'd give you a call.

It's been six years of being yanked around, with him playing games, so why not call his bluff and get him to pay us what he owes — so I called.

You seemed nice enough via phone, so I drove the hour and a half in the rain. I left my kids with some sitters that I knew. I needed help just staying awake for as long as the drive to and from your office would take, but I did what I thought I had to, and I drove those hours on the road. I filled out papers that could have been mailed, and I told myself, it'll all be worth it. If things can get better, and we can finally get our steady paycheck, it will be.

I had trouble finding your new place; it was tucked way back and away from the main road. Really small, though quite clean, but don't attorneys make good money? They ought to be able to at least afford a sign, pointing clients the right way, instead of fielding all calls for directions to an office in another state, but then, who am I to judge? I'm no lawyer.

So little old me, in my wet work-out clothes, having driven all that way, I filled out the papers, and you gave me a pep talk. Best day in court, maybe we win the lottery — get all that back pay, several tens of thousands at this point.

Worst day in court, well, at least orders will be enforced going forward — or so I hoped.

It'll take 6 months of worst case to pay back what's being taken out of my savings, so please understand that I'm reluctant to hand over so much hard-earned cash, no matter the promised outcome. I told you I'd have to think on it.

You seemed kind and understanding and walked me out.

And there I sat again, in my old van, with the seats molding under me. The faint hint of mildew and must floating around me, thanks to the rain that leaks in around the sliding door that my ex once flung off the hinges.

I sat there a while, praying, and I stared out into the downpour through my cracked windshield that I'd hoped to be replacing soon. It looked as though those couple of thousand dollars of repairs needed to keep Ole Bessie running are going to be spent on a shot in the dark that support will finally be paid. It's a gamble — and I'm not one to play the slots.

LETTERS NEVER MEANT TO BE READ

It's for the kids, I told myself. *It's not about you. Never was.*

Suck up your fatigue and your worry and just go for it.

The two, three, four jobs.

The early mornings and long nights.

Those could be gone, if this comes through. If you, dear Attorney, come through.

The living out of hotels, out of cars, single bedrooms, and in basements. Feasting from food pantries, begging for scraps, all while seeing him post shot after shot of him and her on a beach, in Hawaii, on a cruise, then in sunny San Fernando Valley.

Perhaps all those trips around the world, when you and your kids are surviving on food stamps, will come to an end. He'll have to stop posting all those sunny, smiling pictures, and knuckle down, get a job.

And maybe, just maybe, we can move out on our own again. Get our own place, just me and them, how it should be.

One can dream.

I died a bit inside, but I bit the bullet. Wrote the check.

It's like a swift kick in the pants to see the bank account go from so many thousand to less than $20 in two seconds. I could breathe. It's a step in the right direction. Perhaps finally some justice.

Least that's what I told myself. Then, I waited.

A few weeks went by with no correspondence. I thought the deed would be done by now; honestly, I was surprised. I mean, with that many grand, how long does it take to tail someone, huh? I could never do it, but again, I'm no P.I. Got better things to do than stalk a stalker.

Another week or so, I got antsy. I called and left a message with no return.

Another week, and still no word. I had a sinking feeling, and I wanted to squash the whole thing. Ole Bessie's been in the shop, and the rental wasn't covered. I'm further in debt and no closer to grabbing a shovel to get me out.

Funny how prayers work though, and I've been praying. Praying for a sign on what to do, since you don't seem keen on working with me, but yeah, you've got my money, so I feel you owe me. You owe me something.

And low and behold, I get a call tonight. And for a few moments before your voice comes on, and I think it will be good news coming, I'm getting giddy, I'm tasting freedom—

But then I hear your tone, well before the message even gets going, and I know it's not my train coming in. Not today.

LETTERS NEVER MEANT TO BE READ

I almost never check my voicemail, by the way. Too many death threats to skip through that I've kept for records — gotta love the exchanges between ex-lovers.

But I listen once, and my stomach drops. And because of the content, I have to save it and listen again. Then once more. But after that third time, I decide it's time for a drink, and a smoke. I need a hit.

Now, I'm not one for drinking, and I'm certainly no chain smoker, but God, oh God, do I need a break. And with no sitters on call at this hour — I give up. And I call up the only person who would dare listen to me at this time of night — the good Lord — and I pour my heart out.

Why, I ask, Lord, why? Not again.

See, this isn't my first rodeo, and I'm darn tired of being held up.

I had trouble securing an attorney the first go around, too, due to funds. Most don't take credit when your score's lingering around 400, so I was fortunate to find one when I did. But now? You've just received horrible news about your remission (and truly, I am sorry) but your office is closing? Simply closing? Say what?

It's not just sudden, in my mind — it's absurd.

In your message, you assured me I was in good hands (oh, was I?), but that the remainder of my retainer — (my *remainder*? We haven't even started!) will be transferred to a new attorney, a former partner, another hour away, further south.

Excuse me? I'm reeling!

If I want to *not* have my case transfer hands, I need notify you immediately (oh, I will!) and my "remainder" will be immediately refunded. Scratch that. You said, "returned within the month." That's not immediately.

So now... what to do. That's the question, isn't it?

What to do what to do what to do.

Is this a sign? *Obviously*. But a sign to do what? I don't know. Do I continue on? Rally the troops, circle around, or just bail? What to do?

Honestly, at this point, I'm back to just wanting to forget.

Forget him, forget money, let's just all move to Uganda. Start over, no more debt. No more abiding by court orders that were never enforced on his end. No more note takings, and recordings, no more prayers for our protection from him, nothing. I'm just tired.

Funny how "everyone" seems to think us single moms just get all kinds of handouts — sign me up. Free money, free childcare, free housing, free food. God, if that's really out there, someone lead on! I am willing. After working my tail off for six years now — *six* years!

And every year that I'm scraping, he's out there floating by. Cheating the system, cheating his family. Lying between his teeth. And what does he tell me? No one cares.

He must know something I don't — because he's right.

I've tried walking the straight and narrow, playing by the rules, since I know God has a plan. But karma's a little slow, and this girl? She's plumb tired. Tired of fighting, when there is no winning. Not now, and not ever. Not for her, not her kids, and certainly no one else involved.

You too, my now former attorney, have jumped ship, like so many before you who were involved with our case. Perhaps you didn't realize how much hope was riding on your shoulders.

That's fine. I won't blame you. But I want my money back. Forget a transfer.

Perhaps one day I'll be able to afford what it truly costs to get counsel to represent.

I fear though, by then, it'll be too late.

-Grace

VOLUME III

Dear Intruder,

You come into my life, surprised and unannounced. I won't let you. It happened again anyway, but I continue to resist you. You're a pain in the ass but I guess I have to give you thanks. You made me stronger and I became resilient. I was able to handle the shit you wanted to put me through, but you didn't think I dodged it, did you? You came close to making me your slave. I am no slave to your trickery. You may have tricked the innocence you placed in your waiting line of doom. Not me! My mind isn't that fragile, my soul isn't that weak. My body is a shield.

Really, what can you do to me? You can play your game, but it won't work. I can show some vulnerability, but I won't break, and I won't let you consume me and tear me down. I refuse to be labeled and placed on a regiment like all the people you fool to join your collection of victims. Who do you think you are, tackling down my spirit? My spirit is mine and mine alone. It's vibrant, warm, joyful, hopeful, and much more.

You are not allowed into my sanctum. If I could, I would destroy you but that would drive me mad. I would try and hunt you down and still become your victim because of my obsession. That's exactly what you want, isn't it? You sly creature, you made me such a negative person. I hate you.

I'm a happy person by nature. I want to be happy and I need to be happy. Why do you have to intrude in my life, leaving my loved ones to wonder about my actions and words? I haven't been questioned yet, but I often think will you become *that problem*. I need to keep you far away. Stay out of my sights and mind. You're a pest, a virus, a deadly deed.

Be GONE! Stop lurking around and poking your head in my rear view, my blind spot, and the corner of my happiness. I have too much to look forward to; my rainbow of joy in the sky won't fade due to the likes of you. My future won't be dimmed with your presence. I will burn you down with the fire in my heart to stay sane and shine with my everlasting love.

You can't own me. Your deathly siren can't control me. I am not meant to be controlled. What you don't understand, you see, is *I* hold the power. I am more than a woman; I am a beautiful creature of nature. You are my slave, and this is *My Kingdom*.

I AM ME.

To My Catalina,

The wind whips tears into my eyes. That is what I tell the others as we watch your shores dwindle and vanish into the peacock-hued horizon. The ferry, with a cheerful hoot, leads me farther away from you, so far, so far. Was it only a week ago that we first met, my cold feet sopping from the gray lapping waters as I stepped onto your fog-encrusted isle? It is an eternity, as if you had always known me, every part of me. That moment when you enfolded me within your arms, your moored boats nodding reassuringly to a weary and spirit-sore traveler, that moment I knew. I knew I could right myself here. I could be free. I could be me.

I took advantage of your welcome, tramping unheeded on your companionship, happy to take whatever you gave. You gave unstintingly from the wild nooks of your beige-green knolls to the delicate florets of your garden. How did you perform such a magic, so that my blind stumbles transmuted into daily journeys of wonder? These were the perfect days of my life when, without knowing what I wanted, I received love in abundance.

VOLUME III

It is a hackneyed phrase, but a heart *can* break through parting. Mine is shattering like an overheated balloon. All the while, I am thinking, "When will I see you again? When will I return?" Was there a moment... no... I won't ask you that; the answer may not be what I want. Instead, I'll tell myself that you looked inconsolable too at our farewell. Those few drops I felt on my shoulder, surely they were your tears.

I shall notice you now in everything familiar, in the roughness of the round beach pebbles, in the prickly stems of the cactus leaves, in that interminable silver cloak of brume you insisted upon donning each morning. I shall see your soul everywhere and while doing anything I shall be repeating, "I love you, I love you, I love you." I am already saying it with every surge and ebb of the waves that pull me from you towards the California mainland. Now you can no longer hear me say the words to you as I shall say them habitually. It shall be my mantra against the unknown. I am afraid. Glaring ambiguity swells through me, uncertainty swirls around me. Where do we go from here? What course is charted for you and I? You remain mute, unconcerned, while I plot and scheme for ways to return to you tomorrow, next week, the month after. Tell me there is hope for us. Tell me you will always reserve a place for me, the stranger who loves you, to whom you returned self and psyche and life. I cannot say anymore to you; do I need to? You know my essence, and with you, I have never needed words.

LETTERS NEVER MEANT TO BE READ

Always Yours,

Atreyee

VOLUME III

Dear Maggie,

I have never understood perplexity: that state of mind where human understanding struggles to come to terms with obvious realities or is tarred by a certain veneer of misunderstood application, but I finally did today. I saw it in your eyes: the blank stare of emotional horror, the tension around the small of your jaw and the downward bend of your neck. You hardly ever bow your head and so I had always assumed you to be strong, but I seemed to have forgotten. Love makes even the most courageous of persons servants of passion. I saw it today and I was frightened by it. I won't ever want to be at the mercy of my oftentimes aggravating nature, and yet seeing the emotional visuals of my conduct in your face reminded me of how my imperfections have served not only to hurt you but also rendered you miserable.

We indulge our imperfections, we cuddle them, and maybe just when they disgust us enough we try to prune them from our lives. My imperfections have, however, often proven a bulwark to such efforts; as a matter of fact, such attempts seem to extend the boundaries of their influence. But of course, I couldn't tell you that because in some weird way, I felt that showing you the sprouts from which my imperfections emanate will only secure your exit from my life. As a matter of fact, I remember you did in your own way try to make me understand that talking and sharing your realities with the next person doesn't always make things worse and could in many ways understand your frustration at my reticence about the issues I was facing.

Due to the events of last week, however, I feel compelled to in some way help clear some of your doubts so that in some never-ending future the mention of my name won't be a source of grief to you. You may wonder why I have never told you this or offered some sort of explanation and must surely think it an indication of some level of contempt for you and your emotional state. However, you must understand that certain disclosures are not always the easiest to dispense of, and that oftentimes the hardest of struggles lies in finding the right person to share your realities with. I guess someday you will reflect on my person and wonder how we ever got involved with each other in the first place and why it even had to happen in the manner it did. I do understand you will blame yourself and ask yourself why you ignored the warning signs; or at least that's what the experts of human conduct must have in some way gotten to you either inadvertently or through certain actions of yours you may have taken to get rid of the toxicity our relationship brought into your life.

LETTERS NEVER MEANT TO BE READ

I have often wondered where you are. I have in my own little way searched the ends of the earth for you even to the extent of a hyperbolic archipelago, but it feels like your feet no longer leave their imprints anymore. I particularly remember our first nocturnal trips to the rose garden, the one beneath the waterfalls, and how in some unfortunate slip of your feet, you fell into the surrounding pool and I had to find you in the darkness. I think that was really when I knew I had fallen in love with you. Many people do not understand what it means to be bipolar because it is a state of the mind. They do not understand the highs and lows and the seeming frustration at never being able to balance events. Life feels like you are on a surfboard in high tide but with you barely in control. Unfortunately, time and time again, I have come to realize that life thrives on balance, a need to maintain some consistent form of order. And so, I feel I have gotten the worst deal; to be able to love so passionately in one moment and to feel the painful pangs of a spear sift through your heart in another moment — to be swept up in the joys of life and the next moment feel like it's a noose at the small of your neck.

You may not understand what it means to be bipolar and I won't begrudge you that after all; you can only relate with the experiences that life exhausts you with. It is just as much that your fear and distaste for daffodils has often astonished me. I have, however, learned that in some ways, we are all the sum of our experience and sometimes they do not have to make sense. You may probably be in some not too distant place wondering why I couldn't fight it or even try to defeat it. I couldn't because in some way, I was a freak of nature and even if I tried, my self-possession won't allow me; it's like trying to get a fledgling you saw in the shrubs to fly without having grown enough wings. However, there are moments where there is some form of respite and, while you may think it amazing, it is actually my most unnerving part of the whole experience. When I go through a period of respite, that's when I am most charming, adorable, and a joke or two could strike the right cord.

A period of respite is the worst period to know me because in some way you are seeing a very nice version of me, some copy of me you are most likely not going to see sooner than later. I have to deal with it so many times and often find myself wondering why I need to enjoy a moment that will be over soon enough anyway. As a matter of fact, the periods of respite are so little that it barely helps. To a large extent, I thought I could handle this; in fact, I had made my peace with it until today when I learned the existence of something effectively life-ending. So I take this pen of mine to write you even though you are most likely never going to read it. It doesn't matter anyway because even if it did, the Pacific Ocean whose depths the canister containing this letter has made its home most likely thinks otherwise.

-Joshua

Dear Long-Gone Ex,

Remember me? We went to the prom together. I hand-embroidered a huge dragon onto your karate gi so that part of me would be with you when you sparred and round-housed. I tried to help you with your English papers and you tried to help me learn to dance. We were both hopeless.

Remember when we'd go to the Howard Johnson's, the one right down the road from our high school? Cheap rooms for what ended up being high-priced heartache.

I didn't know how much I had lost until much later.

The secrecy, the taboo of it all—it kept things going hot and heavy until the weight of what we had overwhelmed us. You towered over me, a mountain of a man, until the landscape shifted and I was stranded under a storm cloud that hung around for years.

Years.

It's been four decades since all that was us ended, and just a month ago, I prowled around on the internet, staring at your family photos. Time hasn't been kind to you. For that, I'm glad.

Remember me? You dumped me the summer before I was a senior. You dumped me for some tall, lanky girl with flowing hair and legs that went on forever. She was pure. Untouched. You had already touched me everywhere and every which way, so I get it.

Do you remember that after I was married for a couple of years and had a baby girl, you graced me with your presence and your body... again? Afternoon dalliances. Lounging lazily in bed and then hoping your hurried departure went unnoticed. I said good-bye to my husband while you were saying hello to some good girl you met in church.

"But it's okay. We can still see each other for a while. I'm not gonna do anything with her 'cause she's gonna be my wife. We're going to wait until we're married."

I almost made a pond of blood over you. On many evenings, I considered giving up the barely-there grasp I had on life. Nothing mattered except for my daughter in those days, so I continued to live. Eventually, I was able to stand upright. I grew stronger, and these days I'm so fierce, people have to cross a moat and scale a wall to get even close to my heart.

LETTERS NEVER MEANT TO BE READ

I remember you. I remember all of it with such a red-hot rage that if I saw you at an event or if we passed each other on the street, I'd pretend to not recognize you.

"I'm sorry. Do we know each other?"

Oh, we knew each other in ways that made me feel demeaned, that made me feel throbbing pleasure, that made me feel like my begging had no boundaries, but long ago, I read that hate's not the opposite of love. The opposite of love is indifference.

And after all these years, I remember enough that I plan on faking indifference… and I hope it makes you ache at least a little…

Without love,

Someone You've Probably Forgotten

VOLUME III

Husband of a Housewife,

Probably the most hurtful, stupid, thoughtless thing you could say to a stay-at-home mom, a housewife, a work-from-home mom, or homeschooling parent is, "What did you do all day?"

There. I said it.

You come in, from your outside-the-home job, your career, and after only a couple of minutes of standing in your living room, or kitchen, you decide that she must not have done anything all day. Because there are dishes in the sink. There are toys on the floor. And dinner — well, it's on the table, but no one is in their seats, so it must be over with.

So, you turn around, yelling behind your back as you exit that, "I'll be back later. MUCH later." And you leave. You get in your still-warm car and go. She's clueless as to what's wrong with you. Boggled, really. All the kids made it to school on time, and/or to their appointments on time, thanks to her. They got picked up on time, and made it home safely, thanks to her. Everyone's been fed three times at least, most likely more. Diapers have been changed. Tears have been kissed. Hair has been brushed. Clothes picked out.

She's just finished vacuuming the whole house, and in order to do so, she had to pick up the toys, or instruct the kids. She's swept the dining area alone several times throughout the day, following meals. Dishwasher has been unloaded, at least once. Dinner's still warm, and made from scratch, not to mention dessert's in the oven, so double brownie points for all that. The children are done with their homework, which she's assisted with.

They've all spent time outside in the sunshine, and those that needed to practice reading before playing on electronics have done so. The laundry room has seen its fair share of traffic that day, and every day. And all the loads of laundry, the absolute mountains of laundry, at least on this particular day, have all been folded and put away.

So, when you turn tail and leave? She's left questioning, "Why?"

But, even in your absence, life goes on. She finishes feeding everyone, clears the table, puts the dishes in the sink, and begins the bedtime routines of preparing baths, dishing out dessert and cups of water, because she doesn't expect your help, nor absolutely need it, though honestly, it would be nice.

And as she's nursing your youngest to sleep, you happen to come in and rant about how the dishes were in the sink and there were toys on the floor and you also want to say that, by the way, the heavens need open and praise shower down because you, being the saint that you are, vacuumed the living room TWICE this past week and there were still crumbs seen in the carpet?!?

And it was at that point, following your declaration of all you had done (which was very little, by the way — though again, thanks!) that you have the audacity to tell her YOU are frustrated because YOU don't know what SHE does all day?

My God, man, do you even hear yourself? Because I guarantee that, if for even just ONE day, she doesn't do what all she does EVERY day, I can guarantee that then you'd notice. You would (hopefully) notice all that she does, and appreciate it.

Give her a hand sometime, and don't expect mounds of praise for pitching in. Geez.

It's your house, and your children.

And as far as you being the one bringing home a paycheck? Chances are, if she's like most wives nowadays, she GAVE UP, i.e., SACRIFICED her career, in order to stay home with your children. Because of the cost of childcare. Or because she values their well-being and education, or both. Maybe she recognizes the importance of someone being a constant in their lives, in a world where not much can be counted on.

VOLUME III

-Grace

Dear Corporate Bigwig,

Well, it's official. I finally got my first write-up, because I had the nerve to say I knew what I was doing. Because I had the audacity to tell someone, who thinks they matter, *no*. Even though I'm the only person who isn't bleeding the clock or constantly drinking in the office. Yep. That's life.

Here's the deal. You want to know why I'm resistant to training? You want to know why I don't respect you? Beyond the fact that you're a liar, and a good one at that, there are two reasons:

First and foremost, you call us a "team" and yet, I've never actually seen you do anything to help me. Actually, I've been asking for a new desk for about a month now, and I can't even get you to pay attention. It doesn't matter how many times I say that my desk is the first thing people see, or that my desk had seven paint jobs of various wear, making it look like a wooden quilt. You don't care. And I have a feeling that you never will. What can I expect from a company that has a consistent turnover rate of less than a year for every single employee?

I'm well aware that my grandparents think I overly complain about my boss drinking on the job, being late, and leaving early. I'm sure they think I'm exaggerating, even after he slams eight cans of Keystone and leaves at 4:30 in his '67 rally red Stingray. I've even told them that I don't have a second day off and they told me I should be happy with the overtime.

That brings me right around to my last point. Do you know why I don't casually throw respect directly to you? The last reason is simple. You DO NOT need me. Not even a little bit. It doesn't matter how many things I sell or rent, I'm expendable. I know it, you know it, we all know it. The day I step across the line in the sand, I'll lose my job.

Because of this, your training comes off less about bettering me as a salesperson and more about the numbers. Who cares if the constant stress makes me want to put two bullets in each ear? Who cares if a stranger is disrespectful after a second of knowing me and I just want them to implode? Who cares that my marriage suffers from never being home? Who cares that I have a hard time writing or that you're draining my creativity into a dull gray machine that is never going to show me any goddamn love?

You don't. And that's fine, but it means that I'm never going to say, "Yes ma'am or no ma'am." Perhaps that's the spoiled Millennial brat in me, but at this point, that's neither here nor there. Fire me when you want, but never ever make it seem like we're a team, because we aren't.

And that day you fire me, I'm not going to cry about not having paychecks. I'm going to be free again. Free to fly into the sky and spread my wings. I'm waiting. I'm holding no punches.

Hatefully yours,

A. M. Hounchell

VOLUME III

Dear Janna,

What to say after you broke up with me for writing you a sweet love poem on our eight-month anniversary (to the extent anyone older than 18 can have an anniversary measured in months). Maybe I *should have seen it coming.*

Your dating profile stated that after your modeling days you "wanted to be challenged intellectually." Well, that was one thing you said that turned out to be true. You are certainly *intellectually challenged.*

While you successfully transitioned from modeling to a career in business, your profile pictures were strictly from your modeling days. A series of pouting, brooding, hand-on-hip pictures that featured everything but a smile.

You *were* beautiful, but in a way that was almost too orchestrated. Waist-length, dyed platinum hair, porcelain skin, form-fitting designer gowns, and bejeweled headbands. You were like a live-action Disney princess. I'm convinced you were not born, but drawn, likely by a fat, aging pedophile.

Do I wish you'd written a poem for me? Maybe. Do I wish you'd said, "Thank you, Howard, I love you, too!" Yes. Do I wish I hadn't told you that I felt lousy when you ignored the poem, and instead posted a picture of yourself on Facebook, telling the world how nice you looked in your new jewelry when I took you out to dinner? Again, maybe. But maybe you did me a favor.

You told me that night, before I sent you that ill-fated poem with your flowers the next day, that when you thought of the future, you "wanted to be a hot 90-year-old." I'd pictured my 90s like the John Lennon song *Grow Old Along with Me*. I imagined sitting with my wife in a sun-dappled kitchen, lost in our bathrobes, reading sections of *The New York Times* through cataract-clouded eyes. I pictured aging gracefully, each wrinkle a memory of a past laugh. You pictured routine surgical touch-ups, vegan diets, and still-dyed hair. You may have cost me a few nights crying. You may have cost me $49.99 for anniversary flowers, plus shipping and handling. But you saved me tens of thousands of dollars in paying for your future plastic surgery. So, after much thought, I guess I'll just say, "Thank you."

May you marry a man with a microscopic penis and an endurance to match.

—Howard

Dear Sleep,

Sweet Sleep, how I've missed you. How long has it been now? Almost a solid 10 years.

A decade of me cheating on you with life, business, and family. All for the sake of trying to get ahead. And look how far that's gotten me.

When my daughter wrote me a Mother's Day poem a couple of years back and said my favorite thing to do was sleep, she wasn't lying. I completely agree that it doesn't make sense that I've continued to avoid you. Continued to forcefully push you away, with a mix of green tea, coffee, and energy drinks.

Before having kids, while in my college years, when I *thought* I knew what the terms tired and busy meant (oh, how wrong I was), I remember running from you even then. I kept my schedule so jam packed that I didn't make time for what was important — you. Back when I actually had a choice in what time I would arise to greet the day, and what time my head would meet the pillow, I was making a poor decision and burning the candle at both ends, rapidly.

I'd wake around 5:30, dress, and jog down to practice. Run for an hour and a half, then catch breakfast just as the chow hall was opening at 8. Shower and do class from 9 until about noon. Then return to the chow hall for lunch, followed by a quick stint in the gym doing weights before studying and working on assignments — all before one last early afternoon class. Then it was into work by 4 or 5, only to close around midnight or one, several nights a week.

And to think, all of that was by choice! And then the weekends were no better.

Being determined to get that darn degree, but knowing degrees cost money which I didn't have, I took on a second job and cut back on my hours in class. Then I took to working Fridays to close, and would spend the rest of that one night a week out with friends, attempting a pathetic excuse of a social life, only to be out into the morning, serving as the designated driver to the intoxicated and high, and guess who was supposed to be at work first thing the next morning to pull a double every Saturday? Silly me! But it was my choice. Trading beauty sleep for experiences, and swapping much-needed rest for work hours.

Now I'm back at it. Trying to fit in more than the typical 24 hours in a day. Waking early to work out before sun up, then it's dressing, feeding, and tending to half a dozen hungry, early risers that need to be off to school. Half my crew leaves me for the better part of the day, while I keep the more challenging and needy members of my gaggle with me for the remainder of their waking hours — easily the majority of mine, too. **But** after about 15 hours of go go go, I get to tuck everyone beneath their covers and sheets, kiss their tiny heads, then retreat to the office bedroom combo to work until I can keep my eyes open no longer.

At which point, dear Sleep, I greet you as an old friend. And fall eagerly into your welcoming arms.

At least until day breaks and we get to start it all again.

—Grace

VOLUME III

Dear Ma,

It has been a week since we have spoken. When you stormed out of my apartment, littered with unopened boxes filled with my belongings, I expected you would call me immediately. That during the hour-long drive back home muttering to yourself, you would invent new arguments to dissuade me from dropping out of medical school.

I cannot forget the look on your face when I first affirmed my decision out loud in your presence, on the last day of spring break. It had been a long week, cursed with an ominous disengagement between our moods. You could tell something was wrong and kept pestering me about it, and I avoided your worried glare, the lump of unspoken words heavy in my throat. You paused, washing the dishes momentarily, your eyes attempting to conceal an unexplainable fear, then immediately continued as if you hadn't heard me. You wore a helpless expression paired with a disappointed frown I was familiar with, the appearance that had compelled me to abandon my stand many times in the past.

The confrontation followed, around midnight. Just

as the silence had become deafening, you filled the space between us with words, opening up an intense investigation, interrupted with bursts of anger, followed by rational pleas.

"What do you plan to do instead?" you asked, after running out of new forms of protest.

"I will write," I replied.

But you already knew that. Even the finest tricks of disguise fail to delude a mother from the real psyche of her child. You knew that when I was four, narrating make-believe stories to you in bed, using incoherent sentences, and pointing at pictures in the storybook you gifted me. You knew that when I was six, writing a letter to God, asking him to shower us with riches so we could live happily ever after. You knew that when I was ten, leaving a note in your purse, apologizing for how poorly I had performed in a class quiz. You knew that when I was thirteen, confessing that I had no friends at school and I spent my lunch break in the library reading the same books again and again.

I had plenty of time to unpack this week and arrange my possessions in my new home. I piled up all my journals in a neat stack and hid them away in drawers, but not before I read some of my memoirs, spread incomprehensibly across the width of several books. My words seemed too big for the pages as if immortalizing my thoughts as a Tuesday night entry into a heart-shaped diary with a lock on the outside was doing them a disservice.

Especially the recurring tale of a brave single mother, who taught students Mathematics all day to earn a humble living, only to come back home to coach another one, with twice the vigor, training her to break the cycle of struggle that had imprisoned her mother in the shackles of exhaustion.

Even then, I understood how defeated you felt. The constant battle with your financial condition had snatched away all faith from you. But you woke up every morning ready for the toil awaiting you, impatient for the future, where you would live your dreams through me. When I would be successful, your days of struggle would not have been futile. This hope became a menacing notion and, encountering it in your eyes, I dreaded ever letting you down. Felt guilty for having dreams of my own.

It's not that I was ill-equipped to survive medical school. Running in and out of classes, I tried my best to learn whatever the professors had to offer, spending extra hours in empty study halls, tackling challenging concepts. You were evidently proud of my consistent grades, ignorant of the state of mind veiled behind the academic excellence, on the brink of insanity. I was unable to find a moment's peace, tossing and turning in bed during the ink-blue hours, a tide of grief welling up in my heart, making me sick. A combination of alcohol and pills lulled me to sleep eventually, followed by a pack of Camel lights and a gigantic cup of black coffee jolting me awake. I felt like I was disappearing, my body a wrecked ship that I had abandoned. I was transfiguring into a ghost, witnessing my lifeless flesh at lectures, in laundry rooms, and hospital wards. Very soon, I would crumble into dust and dissipate into the wind. It wouldn't be the overabundance of schoolwork that would devour me, but the lack of poetry in my life would be the ultimate cause of my impending doom.

In the course of all these years, I came up with numerous reasons to not write. *It's not the most lucrative profession. I'm not sure which genre I would excel in. It's impossible to estimate whether I possess an innate knowledge of the world so crucial for a writer. Every page I write tastes sour after a day or two — like spoiled milk. It's not worth recalibrating my priorities over stubborn impulses.* They kept assembling in heaps, gargantuan in comparison to the single counter-argument. I had to write because there was no other choice.

To not write was to be dead. It was a compulsion, to craft my thoughts and conceive a present, to wrap it up in metaphors and symbolisms and gift it to readers or myself in times of distress and celebration.

I had never felt this mortal before. The days were pouring in like rain, trickling down my palms before I could quench my thirst. I was inching closer to a defeated fate, identical to yours.

The endless green meadow where my dreams were sown would scorch into a barren desert if I didn't act quickly. I decided to pay no further heed to any indispositions, any obstacles that came between me and my goal to write.

To achieve this, I require resolute and unremitting industry, as well as incessant observations. Every moment is of infinite worth for me for it is the representative of a whole eternity. You have taught me to estimate obstructed fortune and unfulfilled wishes as calamities, when in reality they are necessary tools for a revolution against my present condition. To evolve into a better person, to surrender to something greater than life itself.

You were holding back tears while driving me to my new apartment. On the way, I pointed at the nail salon where I had taken up a part-time job to support myself until I had more clarity about what my long-term plan was. The white walls of the small room were plastered with little notes, tying my new life together in a series of job interviews, writing programs, and loan arrangements. You felt defeated once again, as you saw your worst fear materializing right in front of you. I was gambling away all I had achieved, with no guarantee of any returns. You left before I could tell you how significant your presence that day was. How your arms were my haven in this brutal storm.

Ma, I'm not bitter with you. And I know neither are you. I have taken a risk, pushed myself out of my comfort zone, and you are skeptical of the payoff. The road that leads me closer to purpose will be laborious beyond imagination. But there are no means to conclude this jour-

ney other than to follow my vocation and to repel all irrelevant ideals. I'm prepared to do everything in my ability, to make you a very proud mother. But these hardships
are insurmountable without you next to me, with your
hands intertwined in mine.

Call me soon. I miss you.

—*Your Loving Daughter*

Dear Dad,

I was 13 when I experienced my first heartbreak. You and Mom were screaming at each other in the office. Your other two daughters and I peeked down through the upstairs bannister, keeping a secretive watch as Mom smashed your computer and shattered your picture frames on the floor. Mom shouted up to us, "Pack your bags." I remember packing the most unnecessary stuff — more hair products than clothes, some pencils, and I think I even threw in my hot pink *girls rule* neon sign. I didn't know where we were going or if we'd ever come back. I was 13, but I had wanted this day to come for so long.

I hated you. I hated everything about you.

As the eldest daughter, I was able to watch you transform into a distant and apathetic man, unlike my sisters. I was the only one who could remember what you were like before the drugs. You were kind and loving and made me feel special, like I was the light source of your life, like you were so lucky to have me as a daughter. It made me furious when you stopped making me feel that way. I begged Mom to leave, I begged her to drop everything and take us somewhere far away from you. I begged her to give up on you, and she finally did.

I was 13 when I first saw you cry. As I dragged my bag out of the front door, you grabbed my hand. You looked me in the eyes, for the first time in years, and you begged me to stay. "Please don't go. Don't leave me. Please." With tears streaming down your face, you begged me to stay. I saw my regretful father behind your eyes instead of the usual stranger. Guilt overcame me and I ran to hug you. You squeezed me tightly and I felt safe in your arms. I felt cared for and protected and special. But it was too late for reconciliation. I'm so sorry we gave up on you when you needed us the most. I'm so sorry for leaving you, Dad. I was 13 when I broke your heart. And that broke mine.

With all my love,

Leah

Dear Kat,

Great party at your parents' house on Saturday night. Thanks for asking Ken to drive me there; otherwise, I wouldn't have been able to make it. I just found out my car comes back from the panel beaters tomorrow and my neck brace comes off next week.

If Ken wasn't drunk, I would still be none-the-wiser about you. He wanted to drive me home but, as you know, I'd already been in an accident several weeks before, and told him I'd rather sleep over. I noticed him on the living room floor in amongst a morgue of bodies on my way to the bathroom. Lucky your parents had gone away for the weekend.

Forgive me if I sound rude, but I think you should stop butting your cigarettes out on your arm for every day that Alan has left you. It won't bring him back. I know how distraught you were when he turned up with Lucy. The bastard. Lucky that Ken and other boys were there and made them leave.

Each time you and I have lunch together and I say something about Alan, I hate how you always change the subject. Nothing I say will ease your pain and I dislike seeing your unsightly flesh wounds grow. You know I care because I've told you I do, but not in the way you expect. I had no idea you felt *that* way. It was nice of you to let me sleep in your single bed, but when you came into your bedroom the next morning wearing a see-through nighty and tried to tongue kiss me I was shocked. I had no idea you were bi-sexual. I thought you were still pining for Alan.

I just wanted to let you know that I like you as a friend, Katrina, but other than that, I'm not interested. If you're thinking of harming yourself because of me, please don't. It won't make me change my mind. One day, you'll find someone who loves and adores you. You're a good friend and I'd hate to lose you.

-Melisa

Dear Big Old Tom,

The days of my youth are left in the yonder years, but as I grow older, I wonder if you are shriveling up in your grave, afraid of what the land of the free has become. We are the products of innovation, greed, and religion. Our morals are thrown out the window, and addictions have grown strong. I've seen the good fall to evil, and the evil stand at the head of this pillar of destruction.

If you ask me, Big Old Tom, you would be crying over the mess we have become. There is no bigger addiction than self-destruction and manipulation. Trust me, I know. We are the land of free. But, Big Old Tom, are our stars and stripes worth the demolition of our education, jobs, hope, foundations, loyalty, and dedication to a place consumed with guilty pleasures and greed?

Back when you were a wee little boy they taught you to be kind to women, they taught you to mind your manners, they taught you to accept anyone among our shores, and we fought long and hard for equal rights both as women and as people of other nationalities.

I am your citizen, born, raised, and bred. But I am

starting to see our colors change and fade. I watch as people live day by day, not having conversations and being aliens to one another as the convenience of innovation leads them to choices rather than engaging with the person in front of them.

How are we to win against a black cellular device full of poison? How are to we win when a person can just swipe right and find another lover? How are we to win when the educated are judged by a test and not their own learning abilities? How are we to win when a person walking into Starbucks gets arrested because of his color of skin? How are we to win when the radio only plays explicit sexual songs, and doesn't cater to songs with more meaning?

When did it become okay for the land of the free to give up our title to the land of the ignorant? The land of the ignored. The land of the sheltered. The land of the poor. You can call us whatever you may, Big Old Tom.

My heart is in as much pain as yours. I often wonder how we slid into a society that cares more about what we own, who we see, and what we do, than a society that cares about what we do, the way we think, and how to flourish as individual human beings who respect one another.

Your children are dying. We are being swept into a sea of ignorance and lost into an undivided sense of reality that people are going to want, want, and want until the world dooms itself into a pit of greed. Our land is covering itself in filth from wrappers, glass, and the poor. Is this the world you imagined? Are we the future you dreamed?

Or have we strayed from everything you ever stood for and betrayed our flag? Humans are naturally inclined to betray one another. Have we become what we broke away from England for? Have we driven ourselves back into history, forgetting what we are made of?

Why do people love to drink alcohol? Is it the same reason we forgot about you, Big Old Tom, hanging from our flag poles? Change is inevitable and as time goes by, I get more disgusted by the things I am privy to. While I send this letter, I do hope that you will find it in you to forgive this corrupt society when we are on our deathbeds and we pray to a land unknown. I hope it is you welcoming us to a better foundation. I hope we will see a better world. I hope people will come together, but as time goes by... and more corruption is built... I believe we are doomed to have our stars and stripes stripped away from us, one at a time.

VOLUME III

Dear Obsession,

I often wonder. I keep wondering, and when I do, I become anxious.

When will you come? When will you be with me? I can imagine when this will happen, and if you came, will I be okay? I know I'll be just fine; of course I'll be fine. I'll be more…

But, will you be? It worries me to know you might not. I know my husband won't. If he knew this would happen, I can already hear what he would say and the thoughts running through his mind. It would all be so sudden, even with the amount of time spent in our marriage.

I would change for you, a lot of changes, both mentally and physically. I'm not sure if my husband can handle those changes. Who knows? I'm in it for you. I anticipate the day when I can hold you in my arms, kiss you, see you smile, and hear the laughter in your voice.

Does that make me selfish to want you? It shouldn't. I want to give you all I have to offer. I know I already love you. I want you and I will wait for you.

With Love,

Your Future Mom

P.S. Your Daddy will worry but he loves you already.

Dear Fi,

It's been a long time, and I should probably leave well enough alone, but I need to do this, for me especially.

I'm sorry I wasn't honest with you when I was in Australia, or after. I didn't have the courage or the self-awareness to tell you how I was really feeling. And in case you had any doubts or never read my confessional letter, I was wholeheartedly in love with you.

But I was terrified of how I was feeling, and I felt so guilty for feeling what I was feeling, like I was letting you down somehow by being in love with you, like I was the worst best friend in the world. Only now do I realize that, regardless of how you may or may not have felt in kind, I wasn't the world's worst best friend. I never had reason to feel guilty or ashamed because loving you — in every possible way a human can love and need and want another — was a completely natural thing. And it was true and real and deep.

But I didn't see it as natural or okay then. I'd internalized a lot of negative messages. I was terribly frightened that day I met you in the airport. Elated but frightened. When I saw you sitting there waiting for me, it was like a tidal wave came out of nowhere and sucked me in and I didn't know how to keep myself afloat. It was love at first sight, though I already knew you on some level through our letters and phone conversations. You were so beautiful, more than your photos revealed. And the way we held each other, the way we gazed into each other's eyes after that first hug... it took my breath away. It was like you were seeing into this part of me that no one ever saw before. Ever. And I felt so raw and naked and vulnerable and scared. It terrified me. And I began to know, deep down, what I was feeling for you, what I suppose I'd always felt for you, all those years before.

But I chose to swallow it all down as it started surfacing. Because a best friend shouldn't allow herself to feel that kind of love for her best friend, right?

You were right. I wasn't entirely enjoying myself. You picked up on that clearly. And here's the real and honest reason I wasn't enjoying myself: because every day with you, I wanted time alone just for the two of us, to get close — emotionally and more. I wanted to hold you close to me. I wanted to do more than holding. I wanted to give you every single piece of me. And I wanted every single piece of you. And it was torture to swallow all of that down.

But I had to. I wanted to respect your relationship with your boyfriend (though I was insanely jealous of

214

him). And I didn't want to mess up our relationship.

But it ended up getting messed up anyway, didn't it?

It pained me deeply when I stopped hearing from you. I've always wondered what exactly caused the rift. Maybe I said something stupid in an email and fucked things up. Maybe you just didn't like me in person, period. Maybe what went unspoken was palpable and you were uncomfortable with it. Or it could be that I chose not to be honest with you, as this was the one time I was not, even felt I couldn't be.

There was one night in Oz I wanted to tell you how I felt, to find out how you might have been feeling too, but I didn't have the courage or the language then to attempt it. I wonder what would have happened had I done so.

I suppose I'm writing this more for myself than for you. I needed to get it out, again, with more self-awareness. To send it into the Universe with the hope that it might reach your heart somehow and you would know and understand I was never your enemy. I just had a very real and intense fear. No other explanation. Anything else I may have said back then in a letter or email was just to mask what the real issue had been: I was so deeply in love with you, was frightened by those feelings, and was terrified that those feelings wouldn't be okay with you. I had to keep them hidden. And I felt that way because of toxic shame about myself and about my true identity, which has remained largely buried until now.

I'm not ashamed anymore.

I just wanted to be completely honest with you. I do believe you deserved far better than a letter written some years later, but this is all I've got. You deserve(d) a face to face conversation. But there was the fear you wouldn't be receptive to it, even in writing, even now after all these years. Writing this is probably pointless and crazy. Definitely crazy, maybe not so pointless.

I hope nothing but happiness for you. Though I learned to let you go a while back, there's still a sentiment that remains: no matter where life takes both of us on our separate journeys, you always hold a place in my heart. Those years we wrote still mean the world to me.

Wishing you the best life has to offer.

Always,

Dear Husband,

This is a strange letter. It isn't a rant; it's actually more of a squeak. There are no angry words or imaginative threats. I'm not furious… just thoroughly disappointed.

And disappointment is a whole different thing. When you're disappointed in someone, you're also disappointed in yourself. Is my situation, somehow, my fault?

I saw strength, but there was weakness.

I saw courage, but there was a yellow streak.

I saw devotion, but there was infidelity.

I saw a handsome man, but inside, he was ugly and weak.

Disappointment doesn't lessen. If anything, this emotion worsens. I will live with this emotion forever. Rage and tears — they, of their nature, do abate with the passage of time.

Oh, you'll never read this letter. I'll tear it up momentarily. And these are words I will never say out loud.

217

I should have looked deeper into your character and seen what was there, rather than what I desperately wanted to see. Time will pass. And I will remember my vows, even if you don't.

Your loving wife,

Barbara

Dear Mack,

I wanted to share some things that came up for me today while considering our conversation this morning.

I hate to use labels to describe behavior but then I had a hard time expressing myself without labels. I will try to stay within the psychologists' recommended *I statements* zone.

My head and heart are reacting differently to the situation. My head is like, yeah, it's really not surprising because he's a fun-loving, free-spirited, 33-year-old man. Humans are more like bonobos than Victorians and it's unrealistic to expect a healthy young man to say no to free, no-strings-attached sex. Bachelor party, testosterone, etc. It's completely understandable intellectually how it happened.

Emotionally, it's another story. My heart feels blindsided. Just one month ago, you asked if it would be okay if we started saying *I love you* to each other. I admit this question was lovely and endearing and I let my guard down a little bit. It's confusing why someone would venture into love territory and then 30 days later have sex

219

with a random stranger in the French Quarter without a condom.

My head says the cheating smacks of relationship incompetence. Again, not super surprising. My Christmas present is still a card with the words "Gift Certificate" written in it. It's May. For my birthday, I got a meme text. During a serious conversation about cheating and trust, you floated the possibility of a threesome at Bob's wedding in October. These examples are in this email solely to point to a pattern of incompetence that helps put the behavior in perspective.

Still, my heart is stunned. Cheating was not expected because of the elevation in emotional connection that you initiated. The beginning and growth of love is special. The spiritual connection we have is special. We read each other's thoughts. The word whiplash comes to mind.

I would like you to consider if you are capable of going out with the guys, getting drunk, and not cheating if the opportunity presented. This is important information for both of us. This would point to different relationship outcomes that might work better for you like open relationship, friends with benefits, serial monogamy, etc. Then, I can decide if I feel safe emotionally with someone who loves me and sleeps around. Food for thought.

I've been crying for the last hour and researching "blind spots" because when you have a blind spot, you should expect to get hit there over and over again. You should expect it! I am attracted to stupid, selfish men. I actually thought you were different.

A blind spot is love. When you love someone, they are your blind spot. Being open to love is wonderful and risky. Though anyone can hurt us, only people we love can destroy our faith in humanity.

But I need to work on *I statements*. I feel sick. I feel stupid. I feel disappointment. I feel justified in not wanting to tell you that I love you.

I feel darkness creeping into my mind. Like life was going too well. Whenever life is going too well, you should expect it to fall apart. 'Oh, I am walking on flower petals through a sunny meadow and then WHAM! I step in a giant pile of shit.'

I feel sad. My urge is to take a few days to Netflix and escape into un-reality. It is a semi-safe place because it's a non-feeling space, a place where inconvenient emotions can't bother my mind and heart.

I actually thought there was a genuine connection between us, something that is so rare on this planet. I met you in a crappy college bar, drunk off my ass, and disturbed by the Trump presidency, but hopeful because of the women's march. It was like finding a star fragment in the dirt. But then it turns out to be petrified shit. Not a star fragment at all, just masquerading as something special. Fakery.

But God, thank you for telling me the truth. Of course, you told me after I took care of you all day while you were sick. Making you soup and renting movies and babying you on the couch. Cuddling with you all night. Sharing my bed. This is exactly what I didn't want. Drama. Lying. Cheating. Potential for STDs.

I'm thinking about starting a company that helps people see their blind spots and fix them.

My head is pounding and I feel like puking. Last night was rock star level, back in my 20s kind of partying and just feeling alive. My stoner friend from grad school flew into New Orleans for 11 hours to eat fried chicken at Mother's, see the Radiators at Tipitina's, and drop LSD. She asked me to come along. Rock concert, LSD, and forget about all my issues for 11 hours? Hells yes.

Swaying along with the large over-40 crowd, I realized love didn't hurt me. Love helped me. We lasted 15 months, and it was pretty wonderful. Maybe it will continue and maybe it won't. Regardless, I am truly grateful for the 15 months. Without it, I would have been seriously fucking depressed and depraved since being forced out of my job.

I realized that the darkness is always there. Right to the left of me, in the periphery. It presents like a cliff. But I know if I fall over the edge, it won't feel like a drop. It will feel like a plunge into a gooey pit. I will sink under the weight of it. All my thoughts will be cloudy and dark.

And, it's a choice. I see it and it sees me. I can walk away.

I did get an amazing epiphany, and it hit me in the middle of the show. **Pegging!** You said this was a hard no before, but I think it's only fair that we renegotiate terms. Every time you cheat on me, I get to peg you. This would provide me with a certain satisfaction and may serve as a deterrent for you in the future. That is unless you really like it. That's the only flaw in this plan that I can see.

Though I said I did not want to see you for two weeks, I am willing to cut that time if you are willing to give me what I want. I think I could easily forgive and forget if we take this next step in our relationship. I don't think I can continue to say *I love you* though. I am going to follow the advice you gave your friend Steve, "Never get serious with your fuck toy."

Sincerely,

Mo

VOLUME III

I have to break up. It's nothing you did. Well, our fight did clinch it. You're just a clingy, immature, controlling, nasty person. Me, Charlie, and Skip planned our weekend in Austin six months ago, a whole month before we met. It's a chance to catch up, listen to some Casey Donahew, drink too much, and let loose. I mean, we need that weekend. And to use your kid against me? I'm not even Tommy's dad. He can take him to the ballgame.

By the way, I don't drink too much, I work too much. I only get the weekend to let loose and even that's tied up with you and Tommy. I need to relax. I work nearly 60 hours a week hauling pipe and it's hot out there. Plus, I've got that asshole Bob yelling at me all the time to be more careful. It sucks. So, I don't need you screaming at me about how I've got a baby on the way and Tommy to take to ballgames.

As for Austin, I'm still going. You can't stop me because we're through. It sucks too because I really thought you were the one. When you went in for that sonogram, those little fingers, it felt like we were going to be a family. He's so little and needs both his parents. Too

225

bad that's never going to happen. I just need some time off to cut up. Is that too much to ask? We literally will be in Austin two nights. And once we're there, I don't plan to go anywhere. We'll go to the concert, drink some beer, and then come home. I won't be drinking and driving. The pickup gets parked and the only reason to leave is to come home. Sure, there will be some lookers there, but I don't plan to touch. I have you. Your cute smile could keep me from cheating anytime. I just want you.

Oh, hell, I'll just tell the boys I can't go and we'll go to that ballgame. Tell Tommy to find his hat and glove. It will be a fun weekend. Just us.

Love,

Mark

Girlfriend,

I'm writing this letter in hopes that you are well and in good spirits. I can only imagine the thoughts that seem to trip over themselves in your mind as you try hard to untangle their masses. I am, of course, speaking of your illness.

The first time I saw you, it was in the hospital. I knew after talking with you that you were someone I would come to like and admire. When I learned of your diagnosis, I realized how brave you would have to become. That first week during post-op was hard on you. You were in a lot of pain. The forced cheerfulness you exhibited for the sake of your friends and loved ones did not escape me. I could sense your fears. I remember it was the holiday season and you gave me a gift of perfume for being "a good nurse." I, in turn, was glad to see that you would be home for Christmas. Some time passed without hearing from you. I would find myself, on occasion, reading your gift card and wondering if you were alright. I called you, girlfriend, hoping that you wouldn't be home. I admit, I was afraid for you. Your daughter answered and soon you came on the line. I listened for a hint of weakness or fatigue. Relief filled me, and our conversation flowed.

You told me that the doctors were very optimistic about the outcome of your chemotherapy treatments. I reassured you that the doctors were probably right, yet I felt as if I were betraying a trust, that I was somehow contributing to a false sense of hope. Time passed, girl-friend, and one day, out of the blue, you called. I told you that I had been thinking of you. You called it coincidence because you had been thinking of me too. Our friendship was still somewhat new, so we tentatively traded feelings. I confided my lack of enthusiasm for the job and we agreed it was "nurses' burnout." You asked if I might need a change. I admitted the possibility. We squealed like teenagers when you recounted how the doctors made fun of an old tattered robe you had grown fond of and refused to part with. We labeled it your security blanket, agreeing that we all needed to feel secure at some point in our lives.

You had gone out and bought yourself a black leather skirt, with definite intentions on wearing it out to party. I reasoned that you were handling things well. You said we'd see each other at my hospital in January be-cause your doctor opted to continue your treatments there. We said goodbye, promising to talk soon. I hung up the phone and sat silent. The last week of December, I took time off from work. My days were spent reading, writing, and spending quality time with my small children. I felt like a coward. I was in hiding. I didn't know what I was going to say when I saw you again. I felt like I had lost my objectivity. I returned to work, physically refreshed but emotionally drained.

Coincidently, I was assigned to be your nurse. There you sat, on the edge of your bed, smiling. I smiled too. I was happy to see you looking so well. We hugged in sisterly fashion, just as the phone rang. It was your family. You joyfully told them you were alright and that I was there. I gestured that I'd come back after my rounds. During the day, I watched you maneuver the IV chemo like a pro as you took periodic strolls down the hospital corridors. I took a call from your daughter, who voiced concerns about your wellbeing. It seemed that you were in a state of denial about your illness and she asked if I could be there for you. Resorting to my professional ethics, I advised her to speak with your doctor, giving her the phone number where he could be reached. I struggled to remain impartial, but hearing your daughter say that you had begun to shut yourself off from those who loved you had worried me.

I called a friend on staff in social services, explaining how urgent it was that you receive emotional support and that our conversation remain in confidence. You never spoke of the social worker's visit and neither did I. I took more time off. I knew you were scheduled for more tests on Monday. I called but your line was busy. On

Tuesday, I rang your room. An unfamiliar voice answered. A newly admitted patient had taken your bed.

I assume your test results came back normal... that your chemotherapy treatments are finished and you're happy to be home. I will give you time to rest, to take care of business, spend quality time with your family, friends, and loved ones. Soon, I will pick up the phone and ask to speak to you, in hopes that you'll be feeling just fine. You see, girlfriend, we have a hell of a lot to talk about...

-Anonymous

Alison,

We've written letters before, but never when you were at home, so close by. It was always when you were in rehab or "institutions," trapped in some way — and I suppose this one is no different. There are a thousand things, a thousand moments where I've wanted to say something to you, but you've always been in such a fragile state, and I've always overblown my own importance, such that I was afraid of the damage I could do.

There was a time when I loved you, in that childish burgeoning teen way I think I've explained before. It was weird and silly and one-sided and in those days, you hardly recognized me as being important at all. And then it changed, over time, and I went from wanting to be with you (whatever that means in a 14-year-old's mind) to wanting just to see you happy with your life, regardless of my inclusion or role in it. And that's when I started to feel more like a friend and distant guardian. But the latter role is winning out. It's been a decade now, a whole decade, and I suppose that should feel significant, but looking back, most of that time has been away from you — where either you were sent to a rehab, threatened to end

231

your own life and vanished for months with no contact, or off with your own target of infatuation-turned-love. Roman meant the world to you in ways I can only faintly imagine. There was a time I hated him for it. There was a time I hated him for being a dealer-turned-lover and blamed him for your fall into heroin. There was a time I thought he only stifled you over the nine years you and he spent together.

But then he died. You lost your center, your everything. He was the pillar that held up the sun, and the walls that kept its light from shining. A week before that happened, I asked you if you ever felt lonely considering that the life you led pushed everyone away, and you replied, "I rarely feel alone because Roman is pretty much always with me." It made me think, really think. Once you sent a message to me, saying: "Are you online? I really miss you and I wish things had turned out much differently between us. I don't know if you have a girlfriend now or what — though on second thought, I'm sure you do. I'm a piece of shit, but... I love you. I never knew what I had until it was gone. You're going to think I'm a piece of shit for what I'm about to do, but I can't figure out how to send you a private message like you used to be able to. You are an incredible person and I need help. I am scum. I wish you the best of luck and a happy life. Goodbye, Love."

When it happened, you vanished for half a year, without a word. I, of course, assumed the worst. But this was maybe (because who can keep count) the fifth time you had vanished. My first thoughts were thus: There was a time when all I wanted was your love — and — How dare you die to me? So that was the first time I started thinking maybe it was best if you succeeded, that there wasn't any more pain.

But after Roman died and you started your spiral, as is owed to a 24-year-old widow with more than one addiction, I realized that I could never have filled his role in your life. I did not have the persistent strength of character to be someone's pillar for nearly a decade. I thought I was, on some level, but as you said, *all you had was him and I* — and he would sometimes hurt you. But I realized there was something else. He was always there. I may have talked you off of a ledge four or so times, but there's no telling how many times he saved you, made you smile, provided warmth. Things I could seldom do from far away — in a role I would never have had the strength to take.

The first few times I met him, I don't think you were even there. In those days, I hadn't learned his value, to you, myself, or anyone. He was just the guy who showed up on the day I was kicked out of school for protesting the Westboro Baptist Church — who had been delayed in arriving to scream at students about our sin and employment of queer teachers — distrustful that the school would let us out again, should they actually arrive. We, the ones suspended for the day, walked behind the abandoned sushi bar and sat around. He came by and asked for a dollar. I was naive enough to think he meant to get a soda or can of tea from the CVS around the corner. He used to snort Vicodin that he pulled crushed atop a tape cassette case. He offered me the dollar back, and I waved it off. The second time we met, he remembered me and gave me a pack of Pez candy that had "fallen off a truck" — he had an entire crate stashed somewhere. He also gave me one of those keys that isn't actually a key, but is a screwdriver, bottle opener, and a tiny serrated knife. I used it for years until it broke. The third time we met, it was near the fallen tree behind the tennis courts, and it was nighttime. He handed out road flares and we all lit them and danced in an ominous red circle under the cloudless sky. I kept an extra flare.

I helped set up his funeral, underneath the bridge his friends called *The Gates of Hell*. I told you that when I first saw you, after you got out from the hospital you were (thankfully) in when he died. I never thought I'd breathe easier knowing you were hospitalized, but by then I guess I'd oscillated back to hoping you would keep on living.

I never told you how or why I did it. He was so important to you, and you were in the most fragile place you've ever been in, so I thought it was best to act like I really did care about him. And by the end of it, I did care. I even made him a few things for the memorial, but I suppose that was before all these things about the positive impact he had on you had hit me. I think those things came from me on auto-pilot. As the nice thing to do. A thoughtful gesture. A Pez dispenser shaped like a truck, with a discharged blank inside it, and the road flare, never used.

At first, I went because I thought I might find you there, where plans were being set. In the back of my head, I had a feeling I would find you there, but you'd have taken the quick way down to the bottom of the bridge. But it was empty, nothing had started. So I walked across the avenues and made my way to your home, where I talked with your mother, and she hardly recognized me, having met me only maybe once before. But she knew my name, so we talked. She'd seen it on the letters you kept. And that's when I got the details of how he died and I asked where you were and she gave me this borderline incredulous look as if to say, "You mean you didn't know?"

I went and helped organize the funeral because I knew you couldn't. Because you were locked away, in treatment. And that's why I went. For you. I wanted this to not fall apart, to be the extra thing that pushed you over the already teetering edge. I wanted to hear what people had to say about you and him. And when people hardly spoke your name, and sometimes said "I don't really know her," it shook me. How could they know him, have cherished him, and not know the woman who had been at his side, every moment when your freedom overlapped, and you were out of psych wards and he was out of jail? I hated everyone who gathered there for proving that Roman and I were the only people who even bothered to think of you.

But telling you all of that felt like it would be some kind of betrayal. And I know on some level Roman hated me. I knew from the way he pretended to be you in messages and told me to maybe go find someone else to love — misunderstanding my intentions. He got me, and I really thought it was you. I felt like you thought nothing of me and saw me as some cheap opportunist, some "friend zoned" fool, waiting for the day to swoop you away. And it insulted me so thoroughly, that I, for the first time ever, was the one to cut contact for months.

I often think back to that moment. To what it would change if it hadn't ended. If I had just stayed away forevermore. Where you would be now.

And there are still a thousand things I want to say to you, across one thousand moments, collected. But there's only one thing I want to ask, but need to do in person, even though I already know the answer — precisely because I need to hear it, to hear it from you, because I still distrust your disembodied voice, even though he's dead. And every time I've seen you since, I've never found the time to ask. (Where am I to find the time between mourning and the feeding of addictions?) And every time I've seen you since, and hadn't found the time to ask, I feared it was my last chance. That something — the drugs or your own conscious efforts — would kill you.

I just selfishly need to know. Have I ever really mattered to you?

VOLUME III

What Body,

I sit, I wonder.

I wait, I wonder.

I walk, I wonder.

I talk, I wonder.

I just can't stop, but to wonder more.

Why do I have you? Yeah, yeah, it's all genetics and all from my parents and their parents. Some may think it's God that gave you to me. I don't buy that.

I suppose I can be almost satisfied with you, but I sure need to work a bit more. Who really has a perfect body? No one has a perfect body and they must be ignorant to think so. Even plastic surgery and other cosmetics procedures try and perfect the porcelain look.

Doll? I guess I can look the part, so my dear husband calls me then and now. I guess I'm not fat, nor am I totally bent out of shape. I do work on my looks and physique and I call my flaws. Who doesn't?

I work hard, and I work a lot, more than most people. I have no time for a workout session, unless you consider sex... which, I may add, I do. My jobs require me to move repeatedly, and in ways that *I feel* like I'm hitting the gym.

Pull. Push. Left. Turn. Bend. Squat. Kneel. Crawl. Lunge. Speed walk. Run. Jump. Leap. Hold Position. Sounds like simple techniques at the gym, right?

The only difference between a labor job and a room filled with equipment is the act of performing these movements 8 to 12 hours plus a day. Does anyone spend more than 3 hours at a gym? I think not, you liars!

Anyway, *my body*... for being in my 30's, I think I have it good, despite my flaws. My job keeps you burning and in control. I don't want to overeat, but I do it to you once in a while. I'm a sucker for food, especially delicious, rich in flavor food. I need to watch what I eat and how much I pack it all down. I'm a gainer.

In the last 6 years I have kept my weight below 155 pounds. Oh did I mention I'm between 5"4"- 5"5"? So can you imagine a person being that height and weighing over 155? Very chucky, huh? Oh, and let me tell you, if a woman is that tall, weighs over that much, and doesn't have any curves and assets...

OMG! Flat and bubbly. I don't want to say *FAT*, but this is my story anyway, so *FAT* it is. You may hate me for this, or appreciate my truth, but with all honestly, I do not use the word loosely, and I understand the hurt it may cause someone.

I have weighed in at 125 in my adult years not so long ago... Okay, maybe it was long ago, but I don't aim to be that weight anymore. Doctors tell me it's my full body weight ratio that's important, and I should weigh that much and when I'm not, I'm overweight.

Bullshit! If I weighed 125 again, I'd look *anorexic*. Even my family and friends have told me I looked great, but questioned me, *Are you okay? Are you doing drugs?* Um... I'm fine and no! I'm not doing any drugs.

I do not condone illegal drug use and I do not want to associate with people that use like a religion. However, Mary Jane, I don't feel the same about you. I don't encourage someone to use, but if the person wants it, I don't care... it's natural. I've enjoyed my very few moments with it. Just don't be a bum and not work; have a life and be reasonable.

I've told my husband if I ever find out that he's using, expect a divorce paper with no warning or talking it out. Growing up as a young little girl, my neighborhood wasn't the greatest. There were people using drugs, buying and selling. My oldest sister has dabbled in it many times and for far too long. It wasn't pretty and quite a disgrace. You can understand why I have my policies.

VOLUME III

My body. What else can I say about you? You're my body and I will love you, so don't ever do drugs, stay decently healthy, don't get too bent out of shape, keep your feminine curves in check, and work it!

—*Deun*

P.S.

You'll age well, I agree with my husband

Dear Guy, Who I Can Only Assume Has a Drug Problem,

Here's the deal: I hate you. I hate every fiber of your existence. I hope you are destroyed in this life and every other by a piano plummeting from beyond the atmosphere and crushing you to death.

My job is already hard enough. My boss constantly looks more and more like he's just going to jump in front of a bus. I can barely manage a community with five total staff and with belligerent people barging into my office, yelling about how they have some problem with how loud kids are.

I can handle the constant screeching from people thinking I'm somehow an undercover CEO. I can handle the screeching of my mind, realizing that I'm just another cog in the machine. I can even handle the aggressive screeching of my nails on chalkboard as I try to cope with just how crazy my job is making me.

Then there's you. The jackass who thinks he can just up and steal four AC units in one night. Would you do it if you knew that I was already in trouble? Would you have done it if you could see my face right now?

Probably. If you would just come to me, I would gladly pay you to leave my homes alone. I just want to get good people in these homes. I just want to make my community clean and beautiful, but there's trash like you wandering into my community and stealing stuff that doesn't belong to them.

If I catch you, I'm not going to hold back. I keep an ax behind my desk for a reason. You stole some AC units for meth, so I assume. Well, I'm going to get a little more aggressive. This job makes me wish that I could vanish, not die, not expire, but vanish straight from existence. This job makes me crave oblivion, but I'm not going to chase after that dark dream.

However, if it comes down to it, I will make a new reality for you. I will go far out of my way to teach you a lesson. I'm a stubborn Assistant Community Manager with bipolar disorder, a tendency for aggression, and a literal ax to grind.

Watch out,

A. M. Hounchell

Dear Joe and Diane,

You don't know me, but I know you. You were friends with my granddad. You hosted a weekly poker tournament in your home in the same retirement complex where my granddad was living. Week after week, I would see my granddad and he would tell me stories of his weekly poker nights at your place. He seemed happy. He seemed to really enjoy his times with you.

On the last poker night you ever hosted, something was very off with my granddad. He could not deal the cards. His arm was numb. His eyes and face had shifted ever so slightly. He was struggling. But the stubborn man that he is, he pushed through it. Did not make a big deal about the fact that he had no feeling in his arm. What did you both do? Well, you compensated for his lack of arm movement by dealing for him, ignoring the fact that he was indeed having a stroke. You both chose to do nothing for him at that critical time.

You let him leave your home that night. He dropped all his poker winnings on the floor as he tried to exit. You helped him pick them up and, again, sent him on his way to his apartment where he was living alone.

You had seen firsthand something was wrong with him and you did nothing. That critical time where doctors could have done something to help him, but you chose to ignore the signs. You let him leave.

He went home to fall, lay on the floor for 11 hours before help found him. He had a massive stroke. He is now paralyzed down his left side. He can no longer walk. He now requires a lot of care. Nurses, doctors, and hired help, and Me.

We saw you in the building after his stroke. You would not even look at your old friend. You would both change directions when you saw us. Do you know what you did? Do you know now that you had the power to do something and you chose not to do anything?

You could have done so much like called his family, called the building manager, called 911. You could have informed someone to help him even if he insisted he was fine. He was not fine.

But you didn't do that. You chose to ignore what was right in front of you. You chose to ignore the friend that was in the hospital for 3 months. You chose to ignore the man who is now confined to a chair for the rest of his life because no one did the right thing.

Every time I see you leaving the building I want to scream at you. I see you both getting in your car and I feel such rage. I feel so angry that you are both so selfish. While you are out having fun and enjoying your life, my granddad sits in a chair, alone. I see you carrying on as if nothing happened. You've washed your hands of all blame in this. But I know the truth.

I just want you to know your decisions on that fateful night not only changed his life, it also changed mine. In fact, it changed everyone's who knows my granddad.

I can't blame you for his stroke, but I can blame you for watching it happen and deciding to do nothing about it.

— Tiffany Laurie

VOLUME III

Dear Mom,

It has now been 60 days since I heard your voice, saw your face, or heard anything from you. The last time we were together, you announced to me that you were done caring for your father. You were done with the stress and needed to put yourself first.

What this translated into was that you were leaving this all on me. I was on my own, caring for a stroke patient who is left-side paralyzed and on a dementia track.

I felt hurt when you used our drive home to "quit" your father. I was scared. I knew life was about to get tougher for me than it already was. In the back of my mind, I thought, this was just a tough day. She will come around. Twenty-four hours later, you sent me a text that was a recap of your "I quit" speech. I've heard nothing from you since. So, let me catch you up.

Your dad misses you. He asks me weekly where you are. Why you are not going. I don't know what to say. How do you tell an 85-year-old man on a dementia track why his daughter simply stopped going?

He keeps buying you lotto scratch tickets. Every

week when I go to do his messages, he always asks me to buy 3 scratch tickets. One for him, one for me, and one for my mother. Your pile of tickets is sitting on his desk. There are 8 tickets sitting there now.

Every week when I arrive, he looks behind me to see if this is the week you decided to show up, and every week he is disappointed, and I must go through the gut-wrenching job of making an excuse for you. Only because I do not want to hurt him.

He keeps asking for you to make him scalloped potatoes. I've tried, and I do not do the job you did. He misses you. He won't admit it, but he's hurting because of your choice.

So, I just show up now, as many times as he needs. I work hard for him. I make sure he has food and clean clothes and he is well cared for. I do it all on my own.

Somehow, I am balancing two kids, a job, school, and being a caregiver. I cry a lot. I cry for the stress. I cry because I feel like I am losing my husband in all of this and I cry because I miss my kids and I miss just being their mom.

You dropped your dad, but you also dropped your daughter and your grandkids who did nothing to you. I must make excuses again and again when they ask where Grandma is.

I am tired of making excuses for you, Mom. You are selfish. You dropped everyone from your life who never once did anything to hurt you.

Let me ask you, in these last 60 days have you once wondered how your daughter is? How she is coping with all she has on her plate? Do you even care?

I have days I hate you. I think about you and I wish I could scream in your face. I am so mad at you. Especially when there is hurt in your dad's or my children's eyes.

I have days I feel sorry for you. I wonder how you are. I wonder if you are okay and what happened in your mind that caused you to make such a choice to end communications with everyone around you.

You should know that I will never recover from this. We may one day speak. We may even try to repair the damage, but the truth is, I do not think I will ever be the same. I do not think I will ever be able to look at you the same way again.

VOLUME III

Dear Solicitor,

I hadn't been at home more than 5 minutes when you rang our doorbell.

After picking up my older kids from school and having spent the better part of an hour in the car rider line with two cranky young ones, I attempted to get dinner started.

The chain was pulled across the top lock, so thankfully the children couldn't greet you by themselves. I opened the door and there you stood, having completely ignored the sign to the entrance of our neighborhood that declares in bold black letters, under no uncertain terms, NO SOLICITING.

Perhaps you're not literate, so I'll let it slide, although I'll admit your presence has me searching Amazon now for a bumper sticker to place on my front door stating that this home is protected by both Jesus and a Glock.

I had one child on one hip and two more ran out the unlocked door to sit on our porch swing as you wasted my time with frivolous greetings, and I kindly declined your invitation to insert yourself into my abode.

"Are you the homeowner?" you inquired.

"Why yes, I am. Boys, get back in!"

"Do you have an alarm system?"

"No, and we're not interested, but thank you. Kids, I'm locking the door!"

Here comes my oldest. "Look, a hamster!"

And you exclaimed, "Aw, a hamster? How cute." Then to me, "Have you ever had an alarm system in another home?"

"Yes, but we're really not interested."

And I'm closing the door.

"Have you heard of ADT?"

Boom!

I ended up closing the door in your face.

I'd apologize, and in truth I do feel bad, even now, for coming off as both cold and rude, but then on the flip side, we are a no soliciting neighborhood, and I did politely tell you that I wasn't interested more than a couple of times.

Yet, I still feel bad for not letting you do your pitch, but again, it would have been both a waste of my time and yours, since nothing, and I do assure you, NOTH-

ING, you had to say would have convinced me to enter into a contract of any kind with an alarm seller of any brand.

You see, funny story, back when I lived states away and owned another home during another life, we *did* contract with ADT for an alarm system in a home we bought in a bad area of town. Unfortunately, the police never came out when the alarms went off, and they did go off on several occasions.

The glass break was set off by me dropping a dinner pan in the kitchen. Scared everyone in the house half to death. Then there were the times I set the alarm because I forgot to turn it off before opening the back door in the morning. And what was so crazy was that when the alarm would go off, the company would call first my cell... then my husband's cell... and then if they couldn't get in touch with either of us, or we didn't answer in time, they would call my father-in-law... in a different state.

And why? They were trying to get in touch with us... to see if they needed to come out.

But if none of us answered? They didn't. Wouldn't come out. Wouldn't drive by the house. Nothing.

In fact, this craziness continued well beyond what I would consider normal because, eventually, we moved and rented out the home, but because we were still under contract, we still had to pay for the alarm system for our renters.

VOLUME III

One night, the alarm went off, while the aforementioned tenants were there. The alarm company called my cell at about 10 p.m. to ask if they needed to come out.

"How should I know? I'm not there. Yes, go check it out."

But they didn't. Instead, they called my father-in-law, who was in a different, far later, time zone, and asked him, "Should we come out to the home?" Again, yes, probably. All the while, the renters, who had been unable to create their own passcode to the system for some reason, had the alarm going off. With no way to turn it off, and no one coming to ensure the home was safe.

Finally, they ended up cutting a wire in the basement to silence it.

I, on the other hand, during this fiasco, was trying to reach someone with ADT to cancel the contract, early termination fee be damned. After answering way too many security questions to prove my identity, and more or less 45 minutes on the phone being transferred from automated system to representative, finally, FINALLY, I am told that, no, they can't cancel it, because the alarm is actually in my HUSBAND'S name. And that he would have to cancel it. And where was my husband during all this? Overseas. Working. Unable, and unwilling — who could blame him?! — to waste a calling card on a call not home, but to an alarm company during such a time.

LETTERS NEVER MEANT TO BE READ

Which brings us full circle to my earlier statements, dear uncaring, commission-seeking solicitor: Am I interested in purchasing a security system for my home?

No, no I am not. Not now.

And not ever again.

—Grace

VOLUME III

Dear Annoying Moviegoers,

I wish I could rip your tongue out from between your teeth. Yes, I do have anger problems. And yes, you are deserving. Sure, everyone is guilty of talking during the movies, and most talk too loud. Hell, I talk during movies sometimes, but not all times.

Instead of paying $12 for an overpriced movie ticket to see a brilliant film, I feel as though I spent the same amount of money to listen to you narrate. Nobody needs your constant input. We can see that the creature is on screen. We can see the light turned on. Yes, we can see it, because we're all looking at the same things you are. We're all facing the same direction as you, so just shut up.

This is hardly the first time I've ever had to deal with this, but typically it's a controlled outburst and not the constant droning of some asshole. During horror movies, it is especially bad, but expected. Go ahead, Funny, yell at the screen for them to turn around. My problem stems from elsewhere.

The irony of the situation. I went into the theater hoping to see *A Quiet Place*. It's a movie where people are quiet, and it utilizes that silence, because blind creatures are out for their blood. I don't think you even know how to whisper. Half the time, it seemed like you were talking directly into the ear of your friend at full volume. I sat there the whole movie wanting to yell at you. I wanted to tell you I came to see the movie. I just wished that one of those creatures would dive through the silver screen and devour your soul. It would bite through your neck and leave you for dead.

You're the reason why the movie industry is dying. People don't want to go through the bullshit of sitting near living, breathing annoyances, when they could just watch a movie at home. In the future, when I hear someone else whispering throughout the entire movie, I'll tell them to shut up. If that doesn't work, I'll stop giving theaters my money. Someday, it will be only dumb badassers like you in theaters, narrating their lives despite the movie.

Hope you get hit by a bus,

A. M. Flounchell

Dear Alibi,

You think you can just come in whenever you want, pour yourself a glass of that rich wine, take time away from what we really desire? Fine, go ahead, your work boots are already off and your hollowed-out scenario is already drawn. I get it. Take a seat. No, not there, over there. Fine, you get the comfortable chair with the armrest while I sit on the ottoman and stare into my future. What trinkets have you brought from distant lands to tell us our fortune? What miracles have you discovered in your travels?

You sit and tell of powerful men from foreign shores and their folly. How they make great decisions that are ultimately against them. How they too get caught up in lust and leisure, the predominant forces in the universe. You chatter on about why you know what's best for me because *you* have seen it first-hand. All of this is a parable for why you are right, why you deserve another drink before you continue. I pour, and you make up the story as you go, adding bits and pieces from my reaction. You are not a liar, per se, you are a grand storyteller of the old sense. The problem is, you have no idea when to stop.

Won't I have all the time in the world to play your games? Can't I relax once the day is done? In the setting sun of my life, you can come and ask for your time all at once. Here, take a voucher. Peel off your time for do-nothing deeds straight from the ending. I won't have much to accomplish then anyway, right? In the twilight, I can practice making decisions that don't matter and build empires that will never rule.

Do you know something I don't? Do you know that I am going to die early? Please, spare me your big speeches about living better and all that. You have always been part of the problem.

I talk of others not wasting their time with television, games, girls, fun; meanwhile, I've got a skin-flicks producer sitting right here with his feet up, demanding more wine and a tiny dancer. I'll admit, I don't even know when the day ends and begins. Left to my own devices, I would work and work and work. Sure, I've got issues with controlling my ambition.

I have issues with controlling you as well. You are *not* a tasty reminder. You are the bitter grit in my mouth, just before the morning sun, when I don't want to get up to go to the bathroom but need to. You are that feeling and that taste. The rot. How does it feel to be called what you are? Your arms are tendrils and your conscience weak. The beard that winds around your lying mouth is unkempt, your jeans are torn, and you love like a man of leisure should.

Why do men of leisure make such good lovers? Are they uninhibited by a feeling of strength and purpose, or is that how they define their strength and purpose? Do they have better backs? Do men of work and ambition tire too soon? Do they get so wound up with the worries of the day and their futures that they release before it is time? *Ask in the mirror?* You moron! You wretch that dares set foot in my house, drink my wine, and demand to proclaim what is best for us?

I simply have no time for you, not anymore. I have far too many things to... *who's she?* Why is she turning around and looking at us like that? Is she seriously tossing her hair? Why do I smell Aqua Net? Did you do this? Of course, I get it, you intend on seducing me through her, into living a life of pleasure instead of purpose.

I won't give in. She does nothing for me that I couldn't get on my own. Heck, if you let me follow through with *my* plan, I can purchase through either admiration, or direct acquisition *ten* of her in a penthouse suite in five years. Models, every single one. *You don't believe me?* I can, but not if *you* keep coming around, preaching your nonsense and tracking your mud around the house. Now, get your boots off my ottoman, you've seen the door once... Oh great, now I must clean; nothing is good enough and there's a need for chores before I can get to the real work of the day, planning around you. What have you done with my list?

You hide key items from me to prevent me from completion. I know it, you know it, and just so the air is perfectly clear, I want you to leave. Take her with you; I have things to do. *They're coming for me?* What? Watch your tongue! I haven't heard talk like that since, since... Oh dear, what if you're right? What if they all find out what I really am, and you aren't there to back me up? They say that money and power corrupt — you've even mentioned as much — but I never thought...

Okay, fine. Stay the night if you must... I'll go get the broom. At least then you can testify in court on my behalf and the judge and jury will say nothing of this arrangement. Sure, we can even take a nap on the couch with her, but no clothes, just so there's another *credible* witness. No acts of ambition here. No thoughts of conquering for real, or getting the job done, or feeling a sense of accomplishment. Just sit down and relax...

I just think it's important for you to know, that while I may seem content with you and her, my closest allies and confidants, here on the couch with the games, I will be sneaking out in the morning. Perhaps it's time I do go out there on my own. Perhaps I need to follow your well-told tails and see the world through my own eyes. Your scary visions could be all wrong or you could be misinterpreting the ways of the world. After all, protectionism never prevails. We have our history books to count on for that great fact.

Since that plan is settled and you know what must

264

be done, pass me the wine and let's see what games we can play and what trouble we can get into, *safely*, in the comforts of our own home, all our alibies in check. After all that excitement, I'll just lay my head on this pillow and...

Wait, that's exactly what you want me to do. You want me to make plans for tomorrow, wake up late without doing them, and feel bad for myself all over again. No. You don't get your wish. I have discovered a new secret. I have discovered a new alibi. *Other people.*

There is no one else? Watch it, or I'll call them all in right now. I'll tell them what you've been doing here, and sure, some of them will leave and write us off. But the good ones, the ones that are true and worthy of my ambition and time, they'll stay. They'll listen to my tale for once, about how you've attempted to sabotage this whole enterprise. How your routine expectations of being a commander of nothing is not the way of the world, my world. Once they hear these truths, about how they have come to depend on me and you've stood in our way, I won't need you anymore.

When the bailiff takes me from my pillowed cell and I must stand trial, I will call my first witness, but it won't be you. I will not rely on you to be my alibi any longer.

–Marc

VOLUME III

Dear Lucky,

The phone rang. I ran toward the sound coming from the box with dial keys, a speaker to hear and talk into, attached by a cord.

"Hello?" From my mouth, and then again, "Hello?" I sat on an over-sized, springy rocking horse that belonged to my first-born niece.

A masculine voice responded, "Hello? Who is this?"

I wondered why you were asking that question when you were the one who had called. "Who is this? You called me!"

You said your name. I told you my name. "Oh," you said, "I'm confused, did you call?"

I did not call. I guess both our phones rang, must have been something wrong. We both laughed and got to talking. You sounded like a nice guy and I wondered who you were.

"How old are you? Where do you live? What is your ethnicity?" I asked. It seemed like a lot of questions,

267

but I didn't care. I wasn't used to talking to strangers this long on the phone, unless it was advertiser or telemarketer.

You responded to the questions I asked. You asked about me. I said that I was 14, and that I live in the same city and of the same ethnicity.

I asked you to speak your family's native language, just to prove you weren't scamming a young girl like me, even if it might not be the exact language my family and I speak. Wow! I became thrilled and excited. I started speaking our native language.

"What a surprise, little girl, you can speak it too?" you said.

From that moment, we talked and talked, mostly in English, must have been hours. I would come to address you as *older brother* in our native language. You didn't mind, you even appreciated it. I don't think you had any sisters, but maybe I'm wrong and can't remember.

I told you that I should hang up soon, that my mom and siblings would be home. You asked if you could call again another day. I really wanted you to. I was glad you asked.

"Yes! Yes, you can, but I don't get home from school until after 4 p.m."

After we hung up, I immediately saved your number to the phone contact list. You should have seen the huge smile on my face. At the time, my best friend was visiting, and she sat there listening and giggling. She was a year younger than I was. I wasn't sure if you would call again and didn't ask you what day you would call.

My mother had Caller ID added to our land-line phone service a while back, so I already had your number when the phone rang.

You called again. From that point on, we would talk on the phone for a period of time, maybe 2-3 days out of the week for weeks after school when I would return home. If it was a call on a weekend, we would discuss what had transpired on my days off from school.

One day, you were supposed to call but didn't, and I became anxious and started to think. *What's wrong? Don't you like me anymore? Did you move? Did your phone number change?*

My heart was aching, and I didn't know what to do. I didn't want to cry like a baby. I became busy with 14-year-old schoolgirl homework, and demanding family house chores. I didn't forget about you, Lucky. I waited and waited. I had to be patient. After all, you were 17 years old, in high school with homework, even a girl-friend maybe (I didn't ask, I didn't care). Maybe you turned 18 and thought I shouldn't be contacted in case someone accused you of being a child seeker.

Days after, the phone rang. *Hello?* And Hello back, a male voice returned. Could it be? But the phone number

269

didn't match yours.

I kept calm, "Who is this?"

"It's me; you forgot about me already?"

My heart filled with joy again. "No, didn't forget, of course not! Why do you have a different number?"

"The number you had is my parents' home number. I got a job and I got myself a pager. I'm sorry I didn't call to let you know; if you want to contact me just call my pager and leave a voice message and I'll give you a call," you said.

Automatically, I forgave you. There was nothing to forgive. I was just happy to hear from Bong Lucky. We continued to talk as if your absence never happened.

"Hey little girl, can I take my sister out to eat?"

"Um… where? When? What time?"

It didn't occur to me that we hadn't officially met. I already had a vision of how you looked. Tall, healthy, tan like me, black hair, not long, well-cut hair, no jagged teeth, proportioned, and handsome. Yep! That's how I imagined Bong Lucky.

My mother and siblings weren't really around, not that I was truly neglected. I was able to cook and feed myself, unlike most 14-year-old girls. I was smart, smarter than most teens in my neighborhood, but not the most intelligent. I did my own wash and dry, made my bed without my nagging mother, saved my allowance, and babysat for money, so I could buy personal things I wanted.

Okay, the date was set. *I'm meeting him.* I took my best friend's little sister with me because my best friend wasn't available. She was three years younger. We waited for you around the neighborhood, where a lot of grass was green — out front by the streets, somewhere that could be seen. She got tired waiting with me, so she went back home. I continued to wait.

At the time, there was no Myspace, Facebook, Skype, Instagram, Twitter, or FaceTime. There was email in those days, but we had no computer, as most people would call us "poor."

I didn't feel poor. We had food to eat, clean clothes, money to wash and dry, and basic home and hygiene supplies were afforded. I wasn't poor, I was living.

I saw a sedan circle once before but was unsure if it was you, and the car came around again. You pulled up and rolled the window down.

"Hello, are you…"

"Yes, and you must be..."

He had a feeling it was me but wasn't sure. I was 14 but looked like I was 10. I was a very petite 14-year-old girl. You didn't expect that, but you were exactly what I expected.

I got into the car with you. Yes, it seems dangerous

for a young girl to get into a car with a guy, but I had faith that I could trust you. I'm not religious, but I do have faith. I was right, by the way… you were trustworthy.

You asked where I would like to eat. I said, "It doesn't matter. I'm not picky and I can eat." I chose fast food and we went for burgers.

Growing up, my family always had traditional home-cooked meals. Fast food was a treat, and it wasn't well-known that it could be bad for you if consumed too much.

We talked, laughed, and you drove me back home to the street I lived on.

I didn't hear from or see you again. It was okay. I was happy to have met you.

LETTERS NEVER MEANT TO BE READ

Tired Teacher,

Let me first say this: God bless teachers. I've been there. Done that job. And I'm out!

It is thankless. It is hard. You care too much, and you'll get burned. Burned out, or run out. By the parents or administration? It's a tossup!

We all have our little CYA folders, which end up being bigger than the 2-inch binders we send home with our kiddos, chock full of correspondence that would and will be brought to light when one parent flips out that we're failing her perfect little angel.

This one particular parent hasn't cared to answer any of our calls for a conference to discuss "progress." Hasn't cared to teach their child the meaning of respect and dignity, not just of themselves, but of others. Hasn't signed the progress reports, or returned the "Please Sign" folders of work showing that Little Emmie gives about as much of a da** about her school work as her guardians do.

But when that letter goes home stating that all the F's have added up and she's not moving on to the next grade, that's when Mr. and Mrs. Emmie Lee give a fluff show up, demanding an audience with me, this instant. Forget the other students I'm responsible for — they want that overdue conference in the middle of the school day.

But back to God blessing all my former colleagues. Go you!

Not only are you expected to be caregiver, healer, mother hen, and role model — never mind that you're also probably a provider to your own family, heaven forbid. You must always be a saint, never out drinking, never out smoking, and certainly never in the grocery store making eye contact with Little Johnny as you purchase what every other stressed and time-crunched professional and parent is buying — just say it already — no, not coffee — LIQUOR!

It's as if you have to wear a disguise to commandeer some basic items, like wine, cigarettes, Sudafed, and condoms. Just make sure you send up a prayer that no brown-nosy with the principal PTA president parent is nearby, else you'll end up on the news for your purchases.

Never mind that Joe the SRO/police officer just made the exact same purchases three seconds earlier. He has a gun, for crying out loud, and on Friday night, and he's about to get wasted. But because he's in charge of throwing juveniles — I mean criminals — in the back of his Department of Education-funded car, rather than molding young minds, it's okay for him to have some relief now and then — but how is that fair? We work in the same environment and yet only one of us is allowed a firearm?

I know what I'm talking about because I've had to live and breathe that standard. An IMPOSSIBLE standard. Where I can't lead a horse to water, but God help me if I'm a special ed teacher who wants to keep her job, because in that case I'd best force feed them ponies and hope they pass all their standardized exams. The two months that we took a hiatus on any REAL learning, and just drilled the kids on the types of practice questions they were to expect, yeah, that was good for everyone's anxiety levels. And my blood pressure. No headaches those months, none whatsoever.

So even though Little Suzie has been pushed to her limit all year, as have all my colleagues and all the other little munchkins, and the ones that actually study and do a lick of work outside of what's assigned in class all have straight A's come report cards — it all comes down to this test. And if they fail this exam due to the immense amount of pressure put on them and panic, ka-boom! A whole year of work down the drain. Replaced by that single F, defined by that one three-hour block out of the whole 190-day school year. All that effort. Gone.

Used to be they wanted kids tested for gifted. But now there's no funding in that. Now it's all about special ed. Extra services. And in a lot of districts, what it boils down to is how many hours a day can we spend on the computer?

VOLUME III

We're ousting our own selves out of jobs!

I've been to my kids' classes on days I'm to volunteer, and what I see is hours upon hours of technology doing teacher's work for them. The smart board goes down? We're all screwed! The computer lab's closed? How will we test? It only took 10 minutes to teach a basic math concept? Let 'em loose on the iPad! Seriously. BYOD in elementary? And if you don't, you're left out? Test, test, test more like stressed, stressed, stressed. Whatever happened to dress-up in Kindergarten? 30-minute recess? An emphasis on art, music, and P.E.? Where's all that?

We've outsourced parenting! Gave it over to the government, to complete strangers.

Handed them our FUTURE and stepped back and said, "Have at it! Just return 'em to me in 12 or so years, when they're whipped into shape and stuffed full of fluff." Kind of like Winnie-the-Pooh. Because really, isn't that what's happened? Except no one will get the reference, since it's literary, and who reads books anymore, hm?

When do we have TIME to parent when 40 hours a week, or more, our kids are in another's care? And we're all working one or two jobs outside the home to afford a mortgage, car, insurance, and everything else the world says we need.

Teachers are the new step-parents. They spend

more waking hours with our kid than we do. But as to what morals and functional wisdom they're imparting, I have no clue, because it's not in the parent/teacher handbook. Or the one with all the standards they'll be covering.

And last time I checked, I didn't receive my last paycheck on my ability to write cursive, or recite the 40 something presidents in order, or label the continent of Africa with all its ever-changing countries.

I hear parents praising the start of school every year, like, "Thank God, school's back in session! Now I can get back to my *real* life." Because all summer, everyone's just in survival mode. They don't know what to do with each other. How to be a family. Or how to "teach."

Because teaching can and should take place outside of a building filled with hundreds of little similar-aged strangers.

The system has parents feeling like they're inept at actually teaching their children, but really what do kids need to know? What do any of us need to know? Math. Reading. Writing.

But what else?

Budgeting. Cooking. Cleaning. Basic home and car repair. Communication. How to navigate relationships. Discipline. Faith and purpose.

So, look at this list, and tell me how much overlap

it has with that book of standards they're currently teaching. How much?

To the teacher who's burned out and tired? You matter. Your students matter. But you were never meant to fill the role you've been expected to fill. How could you? You're only one person. The role you're being expected to fill for those 20 or 40 kids each year that grace your class, is... parent. Parents, we need to step up. And you, dear teacher? You may need to step down. Few jobs expect so much, and yet give you so little.

Dear D20,

You have disappointed me for far too long. Soon, I will gather the courage to burn you, break you, paralyze you, and turn you into stone, just like you have done to me countless times. Thank you for rolling high during times that couldn't matter any less, because that helps me defeat chain devils and rabid undead warlocks.

You are my first set of D&D dice, so I'll feel bad, but probably not for long. You can be easily replaced, unlike my character you are constantly trying to kill. I have to be him. He has to be me. It's a *role-playing game,* for Christ's sake, so why don't you try *role-playing* a die that isn't constantly trying to kill me? Or you can *role-play* a die that just doesn't suck? It seems simple enough to me.

Because without my character being attributed to your set of crappy dice, you are nothing but chunks of useless black and pink plastic that I couldn't care less about. So think about this as a symbiotic relationship. If you kill the character, you are only killing yourself, and once you're dead, I have no use for you.

VOLUME III

And I'll be more than just mad if Frylock dies, trust me. I will rain down a hell fury that you've never even rolled against. The funny thing is, you probably wouldn't even be able to escape it because you're a crappy set of dice.

The point is that I paid for you to do a job, and you are not fulfilling your end of the fourteen-dollar arrangement. And I like playing *Dungeons and Dragons*. It's a choose your own adventure story of wonder and intrigue. So don't make me regret this, please.

Thank you,

A. M. Hounchell

Dear Mike,

Do you ever stop to think about how many lives you touched? How many lives you saved? I never really understood what you saw in me. But then again, at that age, I really didn't understand what anyone saw in me either. And yet, there you were, a junior talking to a freshman, and a really young freshman at that. You were my best friend in high school. You took me under your wing and made me feel special. I think you might have been the first person I met who didn't want anything from me except my friendship.

For two years, we were practically inseparable. You really made high school livable for me, and I dreaded the thought of you graduating. I was too afraid to tell you my dark secret.

The truth is, I'm gay, and I had the biggest crush on you. It was like little electrical shocks ran through me each time you touched me or hugged me. God, how I loved to wrestle with you. I remember one time we were in your room, and you were changing clothes. You took off your underwear, and I struggled to look anywhere but at you. I knew that if I looked at you, you would be able

281

to tell I was in love with you, and I couldn't take your rejection, or your revulsion.

When you left for college, I wrote a letter to you, a lot like this one, actually. I was too scared to send it, too afraid that I would risk our friendship. I was sure our friendship would continue, strong and unabated. Alas, that was not to be. My final two years in high school were challenging, in their own ways, and we drifted apart.

I cling tenaciously to the memories of us. They are all I have left. That, and my first, young love that will never completely fade.

I looked you up on Facebook, thinking that some-where deep down you might have been, I don't know, hitting on me that time you changed in front of me. Apparently not. You have a pretty wife and three of the most beautiful children I have ever seen. All of them have your amazing eyes.

I thought about sending you a message, just to say hi. I almost reached out.

And yet, I found I wanted to keep the man I knew and still love rather than discover who he is today.

I know you will never see this, so it's silly for me to even ask. Can you love a gay man? Because I miss you, Brother, but I won't go back in the closet for any-one.

LETTERS NEVER MEANT TO BE READ

Wishing for my best friend back,

-Joe

VOLUME III

Dear Terry,

How could you do that? We were friends. You were my reason for waking up every morning. You were all I saw when I closed my eyes at night. I survived high school because you existed.

You knew all about my depression. You stayed up all hours of the night talking to me, making me laugh, making me forget. I loved you with all that I am, all that I was. But I didn't tell you how I felt, because you had *her* on your arm. It killed me to see you with her, but I smiled because you were happy.

Every time I saw those hazel eyes of yours, I lost myself. Your brown hair, the freckles on your back, those irresistible lips. You were a dream come true. I could fall asleep to the sound of your contagious laughter. I wanted your heart. I wanted you, all of you.

You saved me from the darkness. High school was hell for me. I was bullied, shoved, insecure. People wanted me to die. Remember that? Remember those letters I showed you? I had white pasty skin and so many freckles and no one could ever love someone as ugly as me. I

285

cried on your shoulder while your arms became a blanket to keep me warm.

We lay in the driveway that night, your hand intertwined with mine. I felt the spark between us. Your heated breath whispered sincerities into my heart. I wanted to tell you then. I wanted to dance with you in the moonlight. "Iris" by Goo Goo Dolls was the most romantic song, we agreed. I wanted, no, I needed you to know me. There had to be more for us than online chats when we couldn't sleep. Your compassion wasn't all in my head. Or was it?

You kissed my cheek and told me goodnight. The scent of your peppermint gum stayed with me. I couldn't tell my mom. She warned me that you were bad news, that you would break my heart. She was right. You would keep a tight hold on me well into our adult years.

After that night in the driveway, where you named the constellations for me, we didn't talk much. Why? What changed? I saw you the next morning at school. You had your hair slicked back, one foot propped against the wall, and that James Dean smile that all the girls fell for. You looked right at me. Your hazel eyes burned deep into my green ones. It wasn't love I felt coming from you. It was nothing. I couldn't feel your soul that day. Then, you erased me.

Did you tell *her* about the goodnight kiss?

I caught up to you after second period. I had to grab

ahold of your backpack in order to gain your attention.

"What? What do you want?" You shouted for all to hear.

You. I wanted you. Instead, I said nothing. You heard my heart shatter, didn't you? I did.

"I'm not your friend. Leave me alone!" You jerked away from me and I ran before you could see me cry.

Months passed before you spoke to me again. *She* had cheated on you, made you believe in love, then dropped you. I wanted to be mean. You deserved to have a broken heart. But after school that day, you pulled me to the side. I hoped for an apology that never happened. But, once again, your eyes were soft. You needed me like I needed you all those months ago.

Our friendship was back, with conditions. At school we had to be discreet. If *she* saw us together, then the rumors would begin, and you wanted to shield me from that. I was too innocent and sweet to be subjected to her wrath. She wanted you back, and you couldn't admit that you still wanted her.

Our late-night talks resumed as if they had never stopped. My grandparents adored you. "He cares deeply for you," my grandpa told me with a glimmer in his eyes.

I built you back up, piece by piece. You were amazing, with a heart of gold that deserved to have everything it wanted. She was stupid for letting go of you. I told you that your soul mate was out there waiting for you to sweep them off their feet. I was already walking on clouds around you. I wrote poetry about you, described the way I felt when you walked into the room. My heart filled with butterflies when you spoke to me.

Then, during senior year, it was your turn to pick me up. She hacked into my messages, told the whole school that I was in love with you. She told me to stay away, said that she would kill me if I ever got close to you.

I called you that night, drowsy from all the sleeping pills I had swallowed. A razor blade lay on my nightstand, right beside a picture of us from the Fourth of July. I needed a reason to live. A reason to believe good people still existed. You were my person.

You couldn't come over because your dad took away the Jeep keys. But you talked to me all night, gave me all these reasons to live. You told me how much my family loved me, that I was meant for great things, that life would get better. I had to dance through the storm. Then, for the first time, you told me that you cared about me, that you needed me around. The razor blade found a home in the garbage can instead of my wrist.

The boy I loved finally confessed that he cared about me.

Over the years, we kept in touch through texts and social media. We never became strangers. We were going to have a chance to be together. The day would come where I told you everything. You and I couldn't keep other relationships because we were meant to be together. You saw it too, right?

Did you get scared? You didn't show up because you were afraid of my heart, right?

Our favorite singer was playing a show in town. We both wanted to go, so I bought us tickets right in front of the stage. I left work early to go to the salon. I wanted to feel beautiful for you. But you never called. Never showed up. Never even offered an explanation for what you did.

I waited for you. I sat on my porch steps promising my mother that you would show. Something happened and you were running late, that's all. Maybe you stopped to buy me flowers. A girl could hope, couldn't she?

While the opening band took the stage, I was on my bed crying for you. No texts. No calls. Nothing. How could you do that to me?

I went to the concert alone. For the first time in my life, I went somewhere by myself. I enjoyed every second of Grace Potter, but my heart ached for you. The space beside me was empty, longing for you to be there.

We never called it a date. I never said that word. I just wanted to spend time with you. With the boy who gave me a reason to survive.

The next day, I saw a post on social media. You threw a party, and no one showed. Karma. That's all I replied.

I ignored you for days after that. When your ringtone finally annoyed me, I answered. I told you how much you hurt me. You knew you were just like everybody else. No good. When I asked if you remembered talking me out of suicide all those years ago, you didn't.

My love for you faded into nothing. Hate didn't take love's place, no. Hating you would imply I still felt something for you; I didn't. I looked at you and didn't recognize the boy in front of me. You became a stranger and, because of the pain you put me through, I didn't want to know you ever again.

I'm happy now. I found my other half who looks at me the way I yearned for you to look at me. He takes care of me, makes me a better, more confident version of myself. We're getting married. And now when I open my eyes, I only see the sunshine he brings into my world.

A world you're no longer allowed to be in, because you no longer exist.

You broke my heart, shattered my dreams. I thought I had done something wrong, something to scare you away, but I didn't. You were wrong. You lost me, not the other way around. I wish you the best and, honestly, I hope you find someone who makes you as happy as my future husband makes me. You deserve love, old friend, we all do.

Love,

Steph

VOLUME III

Dear Christopher,

Look at me writing a sappy letter like the girls we used to make fun of together did. Only for you, I'm afraid. Someone told me writing things down helps the whole *moving on* process so I thought I'd give it a go.

Well, to start off, let me say that I haven't smiled since you left. I know how dramatic that sounds, but this was really hard to get through, Chris. You just left. I didn't even get a chance to have a sappy goodbye. And that's why I'm penning this all down, for the flowery goodbye.

When I got the call, I was absolutely devastated. It's like every single colored movie in the world went black and white. I didn't cry, I shook. I didn't sob, I screamed. The worst part? Life went on Chris. People still went to work. They still got in their cars and drove off to wherever they wanted to go. Children still went to school. Television shows still ran, books were still published, and all I could feel was nothingness.

I remember fighting over the best character in the Marvel universe. I remember throwing popcorn at people from the last row in the cinema. I remember your annoying tendency to smile all the time. And that's what I loved about you, Chris.

You were this unique ball of colorful energy that burst into my life and made a permanent home in my heart. When I think of where you are, I imagine peace and beauty. Flower gardens bursting with peonies and roses. Towering dahlias and cherry blossom trees. Maybe even a hidden grotto where you read those sappy Victorian novels you were obsessed with. I imagine you up there having the most wonderful and fantastical adventures. Maybe rock climbing or even skydiving, which we never got around to doing. I hope you're completing that ridiculous bucket list of yours. Especially number seven, plucking up the courage to ask girls out with cheesy pickup lines. That would be a laugh.

Chris, I miss you. I miss everything about you. I didn't want life to go on after you left. I didn't want to enjoy anything after your amazing life was cut short so unfairly. I didn't want to smile or laugh, but eventually I did. I started enjoying movies again. I laughed with friends again with the hope that you were watching. I converse with you sometimes and I imagine your responses. It's like you're right beside me, reassuring me by squeezing my shoulder or patting my head. I started loving music again. I started writing to let everything out. I started living again and I've never stopped feeling guilty.

I know I'll see you again someday, but please never

leave my side. Never let me or your mother lose that feeling of your presence. Comfort her. Annoy me again. Please stay with me. I can't lose you a second time. I really can't. I'm begging you to always be near us. We love you so, so much.

It is true what they say, part of you dies when a loved one leaves Earth for good. I've died thrice now but I feel so close to you. This isn't the mushy goodbye letter I'm writing. It's the first of many, a series of thoughts and emotions, all of which will eventually annoy you. I can feel you looking over my shoulder and laughing. It feels nice. I love you, Chris. More than you can ever imagine.

Live the life you want to live now. The afterlife has no boundaries. Go wild. Most of all, be happy and never stop smiling.

Lots of Love,

M.

VOLUME III

Dear Friend,

Is it okay if I still call you 'friend'? It used to be.

Anyway, it feels nice believing you still exist somewhere out there. This moody loneliness that never abandons me today seems stronger. It's one of those usual, cold winter mornings and yet, the world has never before looked so beautiful in my feeble eyes. The sun twinkles behind heavy clouds, the trees sway with a rhythm set by the wind. The atmosphere swells with this so familiar smell of moisture and wet soil while the sea, dangerously, changes shapes and colors. The world is waking up...

Yet here I am, drowsy under the heavy thoughts that cocoon me. Some days they feel sweetly familiar. But there are days like today, when they reach with their frosty fingers straight for my heart. These are the days I miss you the most. If you were here, you'd know what to do. You would throw yourself in front of the darkness and shine brighter. Why did I leave you behind? How could I think I could move forward alone?

Truth is, I didn't want to end up with my heart bereft of dreams. But somewhere along the way, I forgot that...Will you help me once more, friend? You, my conscience, don't you ever leave me alone, no matter how hard I push.

Nostalgically,

M

Dear Daddy,

I'm sorry about what happened to you in your life that lead up to your final decision. I'm sorry that people aren't more understanding. Suicide isn't the easy way out. You know, I've tried it myself and it certainly wasn't easy. I said it at your funeral and it's still true today. I'm not, nor was I ever, mad at you for what you did. I was disappointed in the situation, but not you. I never blamed myself, although I think I may have been part of the problem.

The world fails in many ways and it failed you. You searched within yourself with therapy, medication, and God, but there were demons eating away at you. You couldn't fight them because you never could find the right tools.

I miss you so much and I try to imagine you in my life now, but it's hard. I wish I had a recording of your voice. I miss hearing you say, "Kiddo." I have your personality and I'm just as goofy as you were. It used to annoy me so bad, but now I treasure it. I wonder if my life is how you imagined it would be. I can't lie and say I'm at peace with your death because it changed my life forever. Your death brought up a lot of fear and anxiety for me. It's made every death I've experienced somehow amplified. I feel pain for people I've never heard of before because I wonder if they were alone when it happened. I hate that you were alone. Even though I don't like to think about it, I picture you lying in bed after taking the pills.

I hope nothing hurt you and that it was a peaceful sleep. I wonder if you felt trapped and wanted to take it back. I wonder if you heard cars or people outside your apartment and wished they could help. I wonder if you heard kids laughing and playing next door. I hope that somehow you put yourself in a happy place. The thought of you being alone is my threshold for emotional pain. You've made me a stronger person, though, and I'm proud to be your daughter. You are forever with me and I'll love you until the day I die. I'm glad that you were my dad and I wouldn't change that.

You used to tell me how much you wanted to find happiness and love. I know it's because you never really did. I'm now actively doing things to make myself happy and to love who I am. It's terrifying, but I know you would be impressed at how hard I fight for myself these days. That's all thanks to you and the lessons your life and death taught me. Thank you for giving me strength and proving to me that I'm not the spineless slug I used to be.

LETTERS NEVER MEANT TO BE READ

I love you,

Your Lucky Nickel

VOLUME III

Dear Claretta,

You and I both know of my condition. It is not terminal, meaning my suffering will last however long I will. No matter how many years remain, I already recognize my limited path in my new homeland. The tropical climate is unsuited for the disabled, and my cane cannot support me through the sand-crusted coastline. The only enjoyment I can derive from the beach is gazing from my first-floor window, where I sleep.

My bedroom is nothing of quality. Formerly the sunroom, I now sleep on a low mattress beside a china cabinet that jangles with the breeze. I have been allowed the luxury of keeping a single window open during the cool nights, despite my relatives' complaints. Recently, Issy and Edu snuck downstairs at night to shut it, but my insomnia serves as a watchdog maneuver. Marisa is not old enough to purposely irritate me, but with those two spawns as her siblings, I doubt she will be able to conjure any feelings of affection toward me.

Appreciate your two functional legs, because you never know when one might get blown off in an attack on your homeland. All of our days are numbered, but I have stopped counting since the accident. Friendless in this new country, my height of companionship consists of the frequent seagulls that sail overhead. They tend to accompany me on my daily walks down the sidewalk, their supportive squawks tangling with the mocking ocean waves. No matter my pace, they eagerly flap with my speed. I am still not accustomed to the cane I was given, and I doubt I ever will be, but no matter how sluggishly I stumble along, my companions follow. Auntie Luiza tries to shoo them away when she occasionally joins me, but they always return.

I am called numerous names. My least favorite is "peg leg," although I do not currently own a prosthetic, yet. Part of rehabilitation is recovering from my amputation, and any pressure to the stump where my lower leg used to be would blind me with anguish. Uncle Danilo has promised to fashion me a peg leg out of wood, once he finds the time, as a metal attachment would cost too much. I am already enough of a burden on them, so I do not need to empty out their bank accounts any more than I already do. My two older cousins whisper indifferent words behind my back, believing I am deaf as well as handicapped. The idea most likely formed because of my reluctance to respond to anyone. If you saw me once more, you would question my odd silence; after all, you and I were the loudest girls back home. Oh, how I hear the laughter of friend groups on the beach. I am slick with jealousy, but it is not their fault for my condition.

LETTERS NEVER MEANT TO BE READ

It is yours.

Oh, but you never felt a gram of guilt in your life, my friend. Whom did you save on that day when gunfire rained down on our town? I did not see you leading the children away from the carnage. Why did I believe the scale of our friendship was balanced, when you were so much higher than I could reach? Trapped between the own boards of my home, I briefly caught your eye, before you turned your head away from me, from your home. Oh, how you charged past the fires, clambering over every soul to save your own. Do not think I missed the little boys you pushed down in your escape; after, they were stolen by a barrage of bullets. Did you know him? Did you not recognize your classmate? How could I have reached out for someone so far away?

Claretta, I know you will not receive this letter. Fate does not work that way, and most likely, my bottle will end in a stranger's hands, or be swallowed by the afternoon tides, never to be seen by anyone's eyes but mine. Maybe your own body has been drifting about for these months, right after a soldier tossed your limp body in. But if the stars rearrange themselves for one moment, and we can meet, then I want you to know that you hold no true victory. You have lost trust, family, and a friend who can never meet you again.

This evening, I will trek across the beach to where the waves meet the seashore. I may fall, or I may throw myself in alongside my letter, but no matter how my end comes, I can only hope yours finds you first.

Once and never again,

— Anonymous

Dear John

(Toothaker D.M.D.),

This will come as a surprise to you, but there's no other way to say it other than... we're through! Why, you ask? The list is lengthy, so *you* sit back in *your* cold dentist chair, angled at 135° with *your* bright light shining in *your eyes* for a change and try to read *this*.

First, your name is ridiculous! Who ever heard of a dentist whose last name is Toothaker? I mean, really? You can't be serious. That's as bad as being called Dr. Pimple if you are a dermatologist, Dr. Fungus if you are a podiatrist, or Dr. Herpes if you are a gynecologist. It comes down to, "It's all in a name" and yours speaks volumes, of which I no longer want to peruse.

When fantasies of your partner drastically change, it's time to call it quits so we need to be done! In the beginning, when I thought of you, I fantasized about dancing white teeth with smiley faces singing choruses of *All I Want for Christmas is My Two Front Teeth* while we did the two-step. Now, after spending a lot of time with you, I have replaced that picture with a horrifying image of you with your hand in my mouth up to your elbow while the song *Love Bites* is screeching in the background. You don't know how close you are to needing a rabies shot with this image in my head.

Your lack of training in the linguistics field is rubbing me the wrong way and I need to get out of our relationship before I do something we'll both regret. How many times did you tell me, "It will only sting a little," only to have a shock equal to electrocution surge through my jaw? I'm glad you're not an OB-GYN because I'd hate to hear what you'd compare with childbirth. And, speaking of pain, if there is such a place as Purgatory, I hope that part of your punishment is having someone cram plastic squares the size of saltine crackers between your gum and cheek and then ordering you to hold absolutely still while you have X-rays combat your skull.

Our communication skills suck now, too. When we first got together, we had light, bubbly bantering, but now, the only time you ask me anything is when you have put two or more tools in my mouth. I guess you didn't like what I had to say because you have almost sucked up my tongue from the back to the front with your vacuum tool many times. Also, do you not know sarcasm when you hear it? When I asked if I could borrow your suction tool to clean the Persian rugs in my apartment, I wasn't asking you a serious question. Duh!

Your expectations in the financial area are absurd, too. Instead of forking out some C-notes and showing me a good time, I have to pay YOU to listen to an orchestrated series of music that includes the sound of drills on two different octaves. The last straw was when you said you'd throw in a score of dental scraping sounds for free. Are you kidding me?

John Toothaker, DMD, we're done. No more dressing me up with cotton in my cheeks to make me look like a chipmunk. No more sprays of air on my drilled teeth (and, yes, I heard you giggle the last time you did it!). No more taking bets with your hygienists on how long I can go without swallowing the saliva that gathers in the back of my throat.

Don't try to contact me from this day forward and don't worry, there will always be someone else out there waiting to fill that great cavity you have in your heart.

Your molar opposite,

Susan

VOLUME III

Dear Donald,

I hear that you finally succeeded in your bid for presidency. Good job, you made your point. Now I would like to make my point. As someone with an English degree, one of my least favorite things about you is your campaign slogan.

Make America Great Again. Let's break down every single word in this slogan. First, we'll start with *make*. Make is an interesting verb, because a country isn't made. A country is founded. A country is shaped and molded, it isn't made. To make something is to create it from scratch. You cannot buy prepackaged cookies and say you made them because thousands of other people touched them already. Certainly, our country is the same.

Make is a command. You are telling the masses to *Make America Great Again*, instead of saying that you will. Perhaps, that is part of a grander scheme that has yet to be realized. Maybe you're destroying the very fabric of existence so that we can see just how deep our so-called democracy goes. I feel like I have no voice, but you wouldn't care about that because I'm just a Millennial.

311

VOLUME III

The next word is *America*. Though I realize that this is a nitpick, America isn't a place. Interestingly, Mexico is in North America. Brazil is in South America. There's even a magic Central America. From context clues, I can infer you didn't mean to say that you were going to make the entire eastern hemisphere great. From your actions, I can't tell what you're trying to make great.

The next word is *great*, which I also find interesting. Great is vague. Like really, really vague. Saying you're going to make something great is akin to saying you're going to make something blue even bluer. Does that mean you'll make the object a darker blue? Does it mean you'll make it a lighter blue? The problem lies in the fact that there are no parameters for great. There are parameters for better and worse, even if they can be argued. Free college is better, for example. Burning everything you see to the ground? That's worse. It's a simple comparison against the former state of something.

Great in comparison is vague and impossible to calculate. If the country was amazing, then great could mean worse, objectively. If it were good before, then you probably made it better by making it great.

Lastly, there's *again*. Again implies that the country is no longer great. Meaning, your aim is to make something better, but you seem to make things worse. In fact, the entirety of the slogan is hollow. It implies that the *audience* should make America great again. You can't force anything, you can't build something preexisting, great is

312

intrinsically nothing, and again is just the catch-all.

What you're playing into here is the toxic nostalgia that racist Baby Boomers still want to clutch onto. Not to say this is the Baby Boomers' fault as a generation (it is), or that they are all racist (they are not), but these aren't slogans. This is a call to arms, and we've seen the repercussions. White nationalists, people who call themselves Nazis, and hate-inspired shootings have come up more than ever. All because of your four-word sentence. Am I saying you created the Nazis? No.

Am I saying that you are worse than that and that you are clearly supporting them? Oh hell yes. Lock me up for it. I'm not about to forgive you for not even mentioning the Holocaust on Holocaust Memorial Day and choosing to talk about your TV show ratings instead. No. You've just been giving racists more power. More and more.

And you are worse than Hitler. Sorry (I'm not really sorry). The thing about Adolf Hitler is that he was smart. His goals were clear, and he spoke as a leader. You aren't smart or cunning. You wield hatred like a toddler would wield a gun. You casually point it in random directions to take away from the fact that you have no idea what you're doing. You're a child with a country. People are afraid to stand up and stop you. A child doesn't always know the repercussions of their actions.

At least I know who can be trusted now.

VOLUME III

– Anonymous

Dear Mom,

A little over a year ago, Pop called me, upset about what was going on with you. He gave me your phone number at the rehab center and asked me to call you. I spent the next two evenings talking to you, working to extract information about your physical state and your mental state. It took some work because of the pain medication they were giving you. But I knew what needed to be done, and on the second night, when a nurse came in, you handed the phone to her.

The nurse was a big help. She followed my instructions and prepared you for transport back to the hospital. I coordinated with Pop, and he met the ambulance at the rehab center. I went to bed that night terrified I made the wrong decision. I had all of these *what-ifs* running through my head. I wasn't a doctor. I had no practical experience with joint replacement. All of the research I did indicated that the second hip surgery was more painful than the first. It was a relief when Pop called to let me know that I had done the right thing.

Emergency surgery. Scary words under any circumstances, but confusing ones when you talk about a joint replacement. There was no question about what I was going to do. I flew out that day. Your surgery was the next. I figured I would be with you for a few weeks, and then I would return home. Boy, was I wrong.

By the time all is said and done, I will have been here for thirteen months, four surgeries, intravenous anti-biotics twice, and helping you learn to walk again with one leg three inches shorter than the other.

This year has been hard on everyone. I have been separated from my own family, while you and Pop have had to deal with health issues and, let's be honest here, me.

Our relationship has never been a great one, not re-ally. From the time that I came out, there has always been a barrier between us. But I'm glad I have been here. I have seen a side of you that I don't think I have ever seen before. Watching you take in the fireworks on the Fourth of July almost made me cry. Your foot was tapping along to the music, you had a wistful smile, and all I could think was this guileless, beautiful soul was peeking through, even after the difficulty and pain you have had. What an amazing woman.

Throughout this year, there have been moments like this. I remember, fondly, some of our late-night chats when you were losing hope that you would ever walk again, or you were afraid that you wouldn't be strong enough to go through another surgery.

What made this really hard, though, was the specter of your brother. His death was due to complications from a failed joint replacement. That specter reared its ugly head a few times. But we managed to get through them, together.

In a very bizarre way, my life leading up to my time with you prepared me for what I would be facing here. My husband was finishing a three-year duty assignment in Hawaii, so I knew how to handle the separation (thank you, FaceTime!). But I was surprised at the other things.

Pop's out of control blood pressure was one. While, granted, I couldn't *do* anything, I could help to guide Pop in tracking his blood pressure to provide information to his doctors. And even for your own low blood pressure issues, which no one but me recognized.

The biggest surprise for me was drawing on knowledge about preparing for a hurricane. We came through that well, too, with minimal damage.

I know in my heart that this is where I was meant to be. I am glad I could be here for you and for Pop. I am also thrilled that I will be going home soon. But, I think more than anything else, I'm glad that we have had the opportunity to become reacquainted.

All my love,

Your Son

VOLUME III

LETTERS NEVER MEANT TO BE READ

My Dear,

There's something I've been meaning to tell you. It's time you sit down and read what's been on my mind. The summer that you turned five, you let go of Mama's hand, left the safety of the cool lush grass, ran barefoot on a ribbon of concrete, and stubbed your big toe. The excruciating pain seemed like it would never end, but as the wound scabbed over, you began to heal.

The winter of your eleventh year, when your mom left her mind and family, you oozed agony. You walked for three years in her shoes. She returned and bought you brand new flats in pastel colors to ease you past the rough spots of stepping around her Southern gent.

Right out of high school, you tripped down the aisle and fell into the mistake of teenage marriage. The preacher handed you his handkerchief to wipe your hot tears and stream of dangling snot. You wanted to run away, but you didn't make the U-turn you should have. You walked on towards an unmapped future.

At twenty-one, completely exposed, you plopped your bare feet in cold metal stirrups and delivered. You waltzed out of the Alaska Army hospital with your firstborn, in a whirlwind exuberance. You followed her around with increasingly bigger Band-aids as she grew more independent by the day.

When you were twenty-three, you birthed a little daredevil who kept you on your toes as he ran faster than the wind and slowed down only to sleep. He hiked his leg over two wheels, zoomed away at three, and never looked back until he crashed and burned at 23 and almost lost his life on a real crotch rocket.

You nearly drowned in your own tears on your thirtieth birthday when you euthanized your fifteen-year-old dog, but stuck with your dead marriage.

Then you tugged your sneaker laces tight, stepped into higher education, climbed the ladder of mild success, and became a teacher.

You and your husband avoided the truth for twenty years and lived separate lives for five more. You finally tromped away from a fairy tale fable perpetuated by the cultural mores of the 60s and cut the ties that bound.

After you kicked a couple of fakes to the curb, you stumbled upon a genuine gentleman. Now look at you. You stride confidently, side-by-side, hand-in-hand, heart to heart with your 50-50 life partner.

Today you will amble lazily with one of your grandchildren. You'll share your wisdom, slow down to look, laugh, and lie in the grass, where it is always softer to land. You will spy a rainbow and tell your offspring's child that the bumps, bruises, scrapes, and abrasions from landing on concrete do scab over, stubbed toes and broken hearts heal, and all things are possible — even rainbow treasure.

Just when you thought your heart and life were full, your first granddaughter presented you with your first great-grandchild and named him after your husband, her most influential male role model.

You are a product of yesterday, but today you can stop searching. You found fulfillment when you discovered your authentic self. Rock on, fearless sister! You've only just begun.

Love,

Mo

VOLUME III

LETTERS NEVER MEANT TO BE READ

Hey You,

It's been a while. I was going through some old boxes and found a few of your things. It's sad that I think about you less and less as the years pass. We weren't together very long. It's only natural that I would've moved on, but little things remind me of you. I'm sure you don't care about any of this — I was always the one who carried you, but I did the best I could for the two of us, and that magical summer we shared will always be a part of me.

So many years have passed since you've been gone. I've learned to forgive myself. It wasn't easy. You left a real void. Still, I learned a valuable lesson because of you: some things just aren't meant to be, no matter how badly we wish otherwise. Our time was a bright moment for me... until it wasn't. Sometimes, I do think about what might have been, just not as often anymore. I've another in my life now whom I hope to love as much as I'd hoped to love you.

You have changed my life in ways you'll never understand. You were my first, after all. Any to come after would be received with open arms, but there will always be that lingering bit of apprehension that fills my stomach at the thought of throwing away something so precious.

Even if I'll never open myself up to feel that kind of unchecked happiness that I felt with you, I wanted to tell you that I didn't let that stop me from trying again. I wasn't the best version of myself when you were around, but, eventually, I succeeded where I failed you. I'm happy to say, I now know what it feels like to be loved unconditionally, though I still struggle to do so in return. What can I say? I'm a work in progress.

Still, it saddens me that things didn't work out for us. I'm sure you'd have been a great big brother or sister had I not chosen to put my life before yours. May God forgive me.

Sincerely,

(Almost) Your Teenage Mom

Dear Mrs. Caroline,

I don't think I've ever been able to articulate the right type of emotion that ran through me the second I found your address in an old box of water-damaged papers that I found up in my attic. I'm not really sure if you live in that same old dusty suburb, or if I'll get this letter back in a few weeks with a stamp that reads *No Return Address*.

Regardless, I had to try. Because one thing that I have found over the years is that things have changed with me. I'm not the scared eight-year-old who would sit in the back of your class in absolute silence anymore. I found my voice and my place in this world, yet my mind always drifts back to the day you spoke with my mother. The day you thought I couldn't hear what the two of you were discussing, because it was a parent-teacher conference, and I was meant to stay in the hallway and keep to myself.

I don't blame you for what you said, or what you did. I used to, but not really anymore. Your words do echo in my mind each time I get the nagging feeling of anxiety pushing against the back of my mind. Because,

Mrs. Caroline, you gave up on me that day. You told my parents that you didn't understand me and that you couldn't. You had tried, and I refused to learn. But that wasn't it at all.

In a way, it crushed me. At that point, I had been to summer school every single year leading up to your class. You promised me that it would be different and that we could try something new. Mrs. Caroline, I was willing to learn until you said that. Until you blew out the one last flickering edge of hope that I had left.

That's a little bit dramatic though, right? I think so.

I guess part of me just wanted to let you know that I'm not really as *unteachable* as you think I am. And you can't make snap judgments on someone just because they don't have the mentality to sit and go through thirty flashcards on the same thing until it's drilled into their mind.

I think I want to thank you, Mrs. Caroline, for lighting that fire under me that made it possible to carry myself through high school with an okay GPA and a lot more experience under my belt. But I must admit, the petty side of me does want to say, "Suck it." I would never do such a thing like that, though.

Signed,

That One Student You Gave Up On

Dear Dad,

It has taken me almost forty years to sit down and write you. There were so many times in my foolish youth that I thought you actually wanted me to be a part of your life. I look back now at that wasted effort and shake my head at my naïveté, my hunger for approval from a man who could never love me in the way that his son needed because I reminded him too much of the woman he loathed.

Sometimes I wonder how my life would have been different, if only I had decided against living with you and the woman you married only four days after divorcing my mother. Would our relationship be better for it?

It all started with her. I will never forget the first time. I was homesick and missing Mom. I went into my brother's room, and we spent some time cuddling before I sleepily headed back toward my room. I banged my head into the door knob, the door banged into the wall, and you both came out of your room. She was angry at being woken up, looking for a target to exact her retribution. Her eyes fell upon me, crying and rubbing the goose egg forming on my forehead. She picked me up and threw me across the room. I landed on my bed, which was little more than a plywood box with a sleeping bag nestled on top. When I landed, I scrambled back to the far corner, trying to get away. She grabbed me by the leg, dragging me back down. She flipped me over and placed a foot between my shoulders, pinning me down. She hit me over and over. When her hand throbbed, she grabbed a library book and hit me with it until the spine broke, throwing pages everywhere in the room. She looked around for anything else she could use to continue. By the time she was done, most of my toys were broken, and those that weren't, I vowed I would destroy. I remember looking at you, begging you to make her stop. But you stood there, watching.

When she was done, she went on a rampage through my bedroom, knocking everything on the floor, pulling drawers out of my dresser and clothes out of my closet. She dumped out what remained in my toy chest, kicked broken toys, clothes and books at me as she stormed around my room. She screamed, telling me that my room had better be spotless by morning, or I would not be able to walk. And still, all you did was stand in the doorway. As she turned to leave, so did you, without a single word. Her last words rang in my ears. "You had better not wake me again or you will wish you were dead."

I was locked in my room, with no way to get out, no way to tend to the open wounds that littered my backside. Do you know how much pain I was in? I was seven years old, Dad. Seven. How could you let her do that to me? How could you watch and say nothing? How could you leave me there, isolated and alone, to face the coming dawn and the hanging threat of her crippling me?

That was the night I learned to cry silently. I knew you weren't scared of her. You stood up to her when she dared to lay a hand on my older brother. So why not me? What did I do?

It didn't matter how well I behaved. She could find some infraction to punish me. Do you remember when she broke her wrist support brace across my face? I still have a bone chip floating in my cheek from that.

The worst though, the worst, was when I developed hives. The school nurse examined me and found all the bruises I, so carefully, kept hidden. The visit from the *authorities* was a joke. They came out and asked you and her if you were abusing me. That night, I truly feared for my life. And you did nothing.

I still don't know what the final straw was that made you kick her out, but for the first time in a year, I had a glimmer of hope. It didn't last very long, when *you* took up where she left off.

I thought about running away. I thought about killing myself. I guess I'm lucky because I was too chicken to do either one. I survived and, ultimately, I got out of the hellhole that living with you had become.

The few times that there has been communication since then, I have tried to talk to you about this. You have looked at me like it never happened, like I'm crazy, or like it was all my fault. I know it happened to me, and I know who did it. What I want to know is, why? Why didn't you protect me? Why weren't you the father to me that you should have been? After she left, why did you turn on me too?

And while I forgive, I will bear these scars for the rest of my life. I can only hope that understanding will make my burden lighter.

The ball is in your court. Will you finally be my father and at least help me to understand and lighten this burden I bear?

−John

Dear Marc,

This letter may be one that is read, and maybe that breaks the spirit of the collection's title, but it can't break the spirit of the concept. First, I want to thank you. Sure, I could thank you for all kinds of things that you've done for me. Like being a co-author with me for a book that I'm proud to have written. Or how you took the chance with a book that's in second person and about a deal with the devil. Alas, none of that is why I want to thank you.

I want to thank you for reading *Running out of Time*. I've probably sold 50 copies total, and even that may be an exaggeration. I didn't edit the book, not because of laziness, at least not that time, but because I wanted it to be pure madness. Like an ancient karate master, you were willing to see my inner potential.

I know that everybody has a story, good, bad, and the ugly, but mine runs parallel to my writing. You've seen my other letters. You know my best man for my wedding and my co-author for some of my oldest works stopped being friends with me before the wedding and I lost something. At the time, I thought the thing I lost was my creativity. It wasn't. I lost faith in myself and, to a lesser extent, humanity.

After that, I wrote *Running out of Time*. It's crazy nonsense that I weaved together without thinking to prove to myself that I could. I needed to know that somewhere inside my heart, I could still access that crazy side of my mind. Originally, it wasn't even supposed to be published, because it was just an exercise of proof. It was never supposed to become this spiraling three-book story with a fifth one on the way. It was never meant to be the work that I was proud of.

Then you showed up. An exchange of tweets because you thought I was interesting. You read the book and you reviewed the book. You restored my confidence in myself. It probably would have happened either way, but I needed you to know that you were the reason. I can't be stopped, not anymore at least. You came into my life on the one occasion that I was slowing down. I was *running out of time* myself, in my writing, and believing in my art.

So, I started that book to end on. That thing you say, it was supposed to be my *magnum opus*. That's why I want to thank you. I went from writing books that didn't sell at all to getting checks in the mail for books that are the top in their category. I went from thinking I wouldn't be able to write ever again to writing a book a month for a year.

LETTERS NEVER MEANT TO BE READ

It isn't much, but I'm grateful.

A. M. Flounchell

VOLUME III

Dear Potential Guest,

Sure, come on over. Anytime.

Give me the grinds of yesterday's coffee and allow me to munch on them with a bitter happy existence while I put a hole in your tailpipe so the whole world can hear what a blowhard and listless extravagance we've become. I'll wake up soon and the gravel in my voice will subside as I yell and stretch and throw last night's dishes.

I'll break out the folding lawn chairs, only to give you a tour right after setting them on that lush grass — at a marching pace to a dead stop — a marching pace to a dead stop — for you to see all my sites.

Then, I'll build a bonfire for you in the middle of the morning to honor your visit. We'll swim in the pond and I'll show you just how easy it is to catch a frog then let it go — catch a frog then let it go — after which, you'll reluctantly pet the slickest skin you've ever put your cheek to.

Drone of early afternoon grasshoppers and the lapping of the waves should put me in some kind of mood that only wet skin and moss can do. I'll chug water from the well's spigot and you'll catch a taste and the rooster will come running with a herd behind and they'll ask about the frogs.

Then, I'll make us bacon over the fire and spot an old baseball for us to toss while I use the tongs in one hand and you'll barely break a sweat.

Before we walk the trail with the Pointer and hunt down berries and big, designer leaves, I'll remember to put my pants on.

About the Writers

Megan Coyote is a 27-yo pagan, permaculturist, mother, writer, and homesteader. She lives outside of Stevensville, MT on 7.5 acres with her parents, 'not-husband', two kids, four dogs, Dexter cows, Icelandic sheep, chickens and gardens. She was first taught to write by her parents as a young homeschooler and, after many travels and adventures, studied Creative Writing at the University of Montana. Now she gets to work from home as a freelance editor and writer, while launching the Diversified Integrated Resiliency Training Center (DIRT Center) and enjoying the hell outta life.

Marc D. Crepeaux is a curator, editor and writer for the *Letters Never Meant to be Read* series. Marc has also authored the gritty, Southern crime novel *Modern Waste*, the poetry collection *Worked Stiff: Poetry and Prose for the Common* along with the collection's sequel *Worked Stiff: Short Stories to Tell Your Boss, and Quintessential Reality with co-author A.M. Hounchell.* He is from Killawog, NY and spent much of his late-teens and early twenties in NYC where he acted like a maniac. He now works as an English professor and a Captain in the Army Reserves, among other entrepreneurial endeavors. He holds an MFA in Creative Writing.

Marc now lives in a more calming environment

with his wife, three daughters, two dogs, thirty chickens, three ducks, one goose, and one Russian tortoise in an old farmhouse right around Rome, GA. He can be found in excess on marcdcrepeaux.com and lettersandbooks.com

A.M.Hounchell is a recent college graduate and newlywed. His claim to fame is *Running Out of Time*, his unedited and absurd novel. He has also authored *Contractual Obligations* and co-authored *Quintessential Reality*. He has two cats, Swarley and Kiwi. Currently, he lives in Kansas with his beautiful wife, Grace.

Frank Kelly is a writer, poet, and photographer, and has been published in local Daily's, alternative press, and Poets Online. He grew up near Albany, NY and has two Master's Degrees.

Frank and his physician/acupuncturist/art quilter wife live in Cortland, NY, minutes away from their three grandchildren. He is an acrophobic who climbed Mt. Rushmore (illegally), a Physical Education washout who once managed an Olympic event, and he's been a farm hand, short-order cook, community organizer, and Good Humor Ice Cream Man.

Nowadays, he prefers working with words and images.

Tricia Lowther grew up in Liverpool, England. A born bookworm with eclectic reading taste, she has dabbled in writing for as long as she can remember. She's had nonfiction published widely, including in The Guardian, New Republic and Ms. Magazine, and her flash fiction and short stories have won or been placed in several competitions, and been included in magazines, websites and anthologies. Tricia was an award winner in the UK's Creative Future Literary Awards 2017. She loves to curl up on the sofa after a day in nature, with a great book, and something she shouldn't eat. Find her on Twitter @TrishLowt

Linda O'Connell, is a seasoned teacher and writing instructor, who yanks, wrangles, and spins words into essays, articles and award-winning poetry. She is a three-time recipient of Poetry In Motion Metro Arts in Transit, and each of her poems rode the rails through St. Louis, MO posted on Metro Link trains and buses for one year. Linda has published regionally, nationally, and internationally in print and online in literary journals, anthologies, magazines, and books. She created Not Your Mother's Book on Family, and Queen of the Last Frontier, a biography which details the harrowing experiences of an Alaska pioneer homesteader.

Linda's greatest writing achievement will be the legacy she leaves her family. She keeps journals accompanied by photos, for twelve grandchildren.

LETTERS NEVER MEANT TO BE READ

A founding member of Wild Women Wielding Pens critique group, Linda is happily married, and is a positive thinker who enjoys a hearty laugh. She has written for monetary compensation, literary exposure, and even dark chocolate.

Her self-imposed writing goal is seven submissions per month, and she writes from the heart on her blog at https://lindaoconnell.blogspot.com.

Meghan C. Rynn was born and raised in Central NY and lived through the great flood of 2006. She then traveled north to the frozen tundra and fought in the great battle against the undead. She braved the 10,000 steps only to take an arrow to the knee. Meghan started writing as a child. She drew comics, wrote short stories, and even wrote a movie script later used for a college project. She is the mayor of a small town called Mari-si, and is the Bug-off champion two years running. Meghan lives in Central New York with her husband and two dogs. She works full time at her local SPCA and is attending college to become a veterinarian with hopes of being out of debt before she dies.

B.L. Teague has been writing all his life. It has only been recently that he has had the courage to begin sharing that gift with others. He writes in his free time, or when his characters gather round keeping him from doing anything else — mostly sleeping, but once in a while doing other things too. He lives on the west coast, though his heart will always belong to the east coast. Learn more about him, and his works at http://www.bryanteague.com

Oeun Sieng Un was born in Seattle, Washington, but spent most of her life in California before the big move with her husband to parts unknown. She is celebrated as an esteemed wife and can handle the propane. She can do any job better than any man. She grew up drawing more than writing, but to tell a story, you must write.

Grace Veritas is a barista by day, vigilante by night. She likes her books to reflect her disposition and coffee- at times dark and bitter, while at others short and sweet.

As a former Catholic who fell *out* of love with the church- and *in* love with a boy- she now prefers to spend her days quietly tucked away in the shadow of Pikes Peak, where she lives with her sister, their children, and their dogs. All can regularly be found hiking the trails behind their home, else attending mass at their liberal- though lovely- church, Red Rock.

She hopes you'll find her stories, like her coffee, addicting. Because really, we could all use a little more... Grace.

LETTERS NEVER MEANT TO BE READ

Jay V. Carter is a poet and occasional novelist from Washington DC. For updates on his work, projects, and perspectives, follow him on Medium@jay.v.carter or Twitter @jay_v_carter

Clara Freeman is a former nurse and freelance writer living in Michigan.

Atreyee Gupta is an explorer of the liminal spaces in which humans interact with society, place, and nature. She is the creator of Bespoke Traveler, a digital alcove examining travel's transformative power.

Josh Lefkowitz has had poems and essays published in Canada, Ireland, the United Kingdom, and in journals online and in print across the United States. He has also recorded humor pieces for NPR and the BBC, and his poems have been read aloud on *All Things Considered*. Born and raised in the suburbs of Detroit, he currently lives in Brooklyn, NY.

Leia Moss is an author. Read more by Leia @ Medium.com/@CaseyDeMoss

Christie Nortje is a 44 year old self-published horror author from South Africa. She has published 9 books since 2011. Follow her on Facebook @ www.facebook.com/christie.nortje.

Joshua Ogri is a freelance and content writer. He also blogs at winnersroadmap.

Leah Oviedo is a writer and artist living in Southern California who loves to travel. Her writing career began in 2011 while working at a center for victims of domestic violence and sexual assault. Through her training, she was inspired to write about women's rights, mental illness, and social justice.

Konstantina P. can be found on her blog @ konstantinasays.wordpress.com

Barbara Pengelly had three diverse careers before choosing to write fiction: First, as an artist selling in Mid-Atlantic venues, then as communications director for a Pennsylvania software company, and finally, as a forensic document specialist, authenticating, buying and selling historic autographs and rare documents. The MWA has published her work including, "Finding Your Stumbles" and "75 Below." She currently lives in a small town in Western Maryland where she is working on a self-help book about autograph collecting, as well as a novel. Look for her collection of short stories to be out later this year, courtesy of Rusty Wheels Media.

Tina Rafowitz is a freelance writer in Minneapolis, Minnesota, she writes mostly nonfiction essays.

Jean Reyes is a SDSCPA Creative Writing Major

LETTERS NEVER MEANT TO BE READ

If you enjoyed this book, please be sure to review and check out these other titles from the Catalog of Rusty Wheels Media, LLC. or visit Lettersandbooks.com

Stop That Wedding

Quintessential Reality

Letters Never Meant to be Read (Volume II)

Letters Never Meant to be Read (Volume I)

Contractual Obligations

Worked Stiff: Poetry and Prose for the Common

Worked Stiff: Short Stories to Tell Your Boss

Where Did You Go?: A 21st Century Guide to Finding Yourself Again

The Forge: Certified Six Sigma Green Belt Certification Program Workbook

As Always,

If you have any letters of your own, send them to us, signed or anonymous correspondence will always be considered for the collection...

lettersnever@lettersandbooks.com

or

Rusty Wheels Media, LLC

PO Box 1692

Rome, GA 30162

Lettersandbooks.com